$\int$ONG *of*
$\int$URVIVAL

Song *of* Survival

Women Interned

Helen Colijn

White Cloud Press
Ashland, Oregon

99 98 97   5 4 3 2 1

Cover design by Impact Graphics
Cover photograph © Twentieth Century Fox. All rights reserved.
Photograph of Helen Colijn by Alice Grulich-Jones
Printed in Canada
Cloth edition published 1995, ISBN 1-883991-10-2
Paper edition published 1997, ISBN 1-883991-14-5

Photography credits: Unless otherwise noted, photographs are from the personal collection of Helen Colijn

LIBRARY OF CONGRESS CATALOGING IN PUBLICATION DATA

Colijn, Helen.
Song of Survival : women interned / by Helen Colijn
p.   cm.
Includes bibliographical references and index
ISBN 1-883991-14-5
1. Colijn, Helen. 2. World War, 1939-1945--Prisoners and prisons, Japanese.
3. World War, 1939-1945--Personal narratives, Dutch.
4. Women prisoners--Indonesia--Sumatra--Biography.
5. Prisoners of war--Indonesia--Sumatra.
6. World War, 1939-1945--Music of the war.
7. Sumatra (Indonesia)--History. I. Title.
D805.I55C66   1995
940.54'7252--dc20
95-33399
CIP

Index

NATOMAS

TABLE OF CONTENTS

This book takes its title from extraordinary music created during the second world war in a women's prison camp. In actual time, the music fills only a small part of the story. The women had to assemble first, by dramatic ways, on the tropical island where the camp was located. Camp conditions had to become really bad before the women, to lift low spirits, thought up their novel musical idea. But the impact of the music was tremendous, and is again, now that the music is sung in countries around the world.

All events in this book really took place. All persons really existed. But in some cases, to protect people's privacy, I have used fictional first names only.

Instead of weaving more informative details into the text or adding footnotes or endnotes, I have included helpful information on geography, customs, and languages at the back of the book, beginning on page 201. On page 203 I explain my feelings about calling the Japanese anything other than Japanese.

*Dedicated to Antoinette and Alette,
and to the memory of our parents*

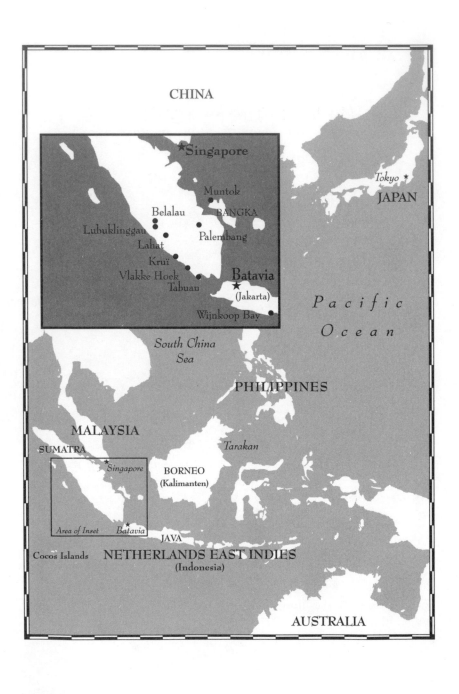

Chapter One

Escape from Tarakan

N ear the east coast of the big island of Borneo in Southeast Asia lies a fleck of an island called Tarakan. It is covered by jungle, except for an area where the oil derricks stand and the people live who conduct the business of pumping Tarakan's oil.

Living on the little island in 1941, when Tarakan was part of the Netherlands East Indies, were my mother Aaltje (Zus) Colijn and my father Anton Colijn, manager of the Bataafsche Petroleum Maatschappij (BPM) oil facility, a Dutch company of the Shell group.

In 1939, when we had finished high school in the Netherlands, my parents invited my sister Antoinette and me for a three-month visit to see them and "become acquainted with the tropical part of the Netherlands realm." After the visit, we were to return home for further studies. But World War II disrupted our plans and our lives. In September 1939, the Germans invaded Poland. In May 1940, they invaded The Netherlands.

Antoinette and I did not go back, but stayed on in Batavia (now called Jakarta) on the island of Java. For the first time, we were on our own. We lived in a rented cottage with Sitih, a Javanese woman who cleaned house, marketed, and cooked for us.

1

We needed to earn a living. I took courses at a secretarial school and landed a job as secretary at the Governor-General's Cabinet. Antoinette worked toward getting her accreditation as a teacher in the Mensendieck system of shaping posture and thus releasing muscular discomfort.

In the fall of 1941, when I was 20 and Antoinette 19, we joined our parents again on Tarakan. We were disappointed that our fifteen-year-old sister Alette could not join us. She was still attending high school in the mountain town of Bandung on Java, boarding there with a Dutch family.

Because of Father's BPM assignments to remote posts, where we girls couldn't follow, our family get-togethers were precious to us. We remembered with pleasure our reunions in The Hague, where we had frolicked in the North Sea near our house. Mother always had hot chocolate ready upon our return. In those days, we had ridden on rented horses, walked in the coastal sand dunes, skated on Holland's canals, skied in the Alps, hiked alpine mountain trails, or climbed rocky pinnacles and glacier-covered peaks. Father believed in *mens sana in corpore sano*—a healthy mind in a healthy body—and sports were fine for building health and character.

And so it was no surprise, when we arrived in Tarakan, to see next to the bougainvillaeas a rack with a climbing rope and rings and a cinder track where we could throw the discus and the javelin. And every evening after dinner we took long walks.

A black-out was in force. Tarakan's military authorities feared that Japan would enter the war and that Tarakan would be the first spot attacked. So the streets were without lights. The houses looked dead and forbidding, all light and life inside closed off by black-out curtains.

In contrast to this death-like atmosphere, our parents walked briskly, business-as-usual. Father walked in Bermuda shorts and his favorite cotton shirt that "best absorbed perspiration." Mother walked in one of her cotton dresses, custom-made by a Chinese tailor on Java. Occasionally she would pat her brow with one of her dainty embroidered handkerchiefs, dabbed with a drop of her *Aimant* perfume.

Beyond the houses we walked on dirt roads cut through the jungle, where all kinds of mysterious creatures rustled, hissed, and screeched. And everywhere, eerily, oil pumps nodded their heads, "Yes, yes, yes." Yes to doom, I thought.

Father explained, "What you have to realize is that Japan needs oil,

My mother Zus on a boat trip off Tarakan a year before Japan attacked the island.

My father Anton a few years earlier on a sailing outing in Holland.

and we have plenty of this beautiful stuff here. It doesn't even have to be refined. You can just use it in a ship as it is pumped from the soil. Japan is not going to bypass Tarakan."

I was relieved to leave that gloomy place and return to a less oppressive atmosphere in Batavia. Antoinette reprimanded me, "Of course, it was a gloomy place, but concentrate on the good parts of the visit. We saw a lot of Father and Mother. We don't know when we'll see them again."

In Batavia we talked about whether Mother should have left Tarakan and come to Java, as most of the other company wives did. Father had suggested this, but Mother had said resolutely that she had volunteered to work as a Red Cross nurse on Tarakan. She had a task here, she would stay.

Then Tarakan was attacked, just a month after Japan attacked Pearl Harbor and the Dutch government-in-exile in London declared war on Japan. A huge Japanese fleet came steaming down from the Philippines with an invasion force of an estimated 20,000 men. The Royal Netherlands East Indies Army garrison on Tarakan numbered only 1,300. Some were professional soldiers, others reserve, like Father.

After only two days, on January 13, 1942, the little Dutch force had to surrender, but it still managed to carry out a preplanned "scorched-earth policy" intended to keep all valuable resources and equipment out of en-

3

emy hands. Seven hundred oil wells were dynamited. All the enormous oil tanks were set afire, and oil flowed in fiery streams to the sea, where two days later it still burned.

After Tarakan's surrender, my sisters and I on Java made frantic inquiries at official bureaus. What exactly had happened on Tarakan, what was going on now. But Tarakan seemed to be hermetically sealed off from the rest of the world. No one knew anything. When finally we did receive news, it was startling and very scary.

The Japanese were furious to see the precious oil they came for go up in flames. They took Mother and the other nurses as prisoners, ignoring their neutral status as Red Cross volunteers. Father, who had fought as an officer with the Army, and another Dutch officer were taken hostage. They were sent under Japanese guard on a small BPM ship on a diabolic mission to Balik-Papan on Borneo, another BPM facility south of Tarakan. Father had to hand over a Japanese document to the Dutch in charge there. The message was: if they dared to destroy the oil, as the Dutch had done on Tarakan, the women prisoners on Tarakan, including my mother, would be executed.

But when a Dutch Navy plane flew over the boat, Father and his compatriot saw their chance. The two hostages talked their Japanese guards, who were drunk, into stepping out of sight into the little lounge. Then they quickly locked the door, ran to the deck, and began waving to the plane with a towel. As the plane prepared to land, the two men jumped overboard. The plane splashed down on the water, the hostages were pulled inside, and flew to Balik-Papan as free men.

Of course, the Balik-Papan oil was destroyed in the same scorched-earth policy in effect on Tarakan. What happened to his wife and the other women prisoners on Tarakan, Father never found out.

After he was flown to Java and assigned to Royal Netherlands East Indies Army headquarters in Bandung, Father stunned us with phone calls. The seal on Tarakan was broken. Father was driven in a military car to Batavia. In our blacked-out cottage, he told Antoinette and me about the battle of Tarakan, and how he had to leave Mother behind in Japanese hands. "But at least they gave me permission to say good-bye to her before I was sent to Balik-Papan. We were able to pray together."

In a modest way my sisters and I now participated in the defense of

Antoinette, Helen, and Alette at their parents' home two years before the Japanese attack on the Netherlands East Indies.

Java. It was to be the last stronghold of the defense. Maybe, with Allied help, it could be held. Antoinette and I joined a newly formed Women's Auto Corps (VAC), which dressed in snappy khakis and dashing pith helmets. I soon dropped out so I could be on call for the coding and decoding of telegrams at my workplace, but Antoinette learned to drive trucks and fire engines.

We followed civil defense instructions and placed a sturdy "bomb table" in our living room, to hide under in case of enemy air attack. Under the table we stacked cans of food. But we never sat under the table or ate any of the emergency rations.

In Bandung, Alette dutifully went to her school, a *lyceum*. After school she donned the khaki uniform of the "Orange Youth" organization and, with other students, worked a switchboard in an air raid protection center.

The war went badly for the Royal Netherlands East Indies Army and hastily assembled Allied forces. Japan had too much of everything—planes, ships, well-trained soldiers. They occupied the outer islands one by one, sinking most of the combined American, British, Dutch, and Australian fleet sent out to protect Java.

On February 21, 1942, the Governor-General left his palace in Batavia and, accompanied by high government officials, traveled in a procession of automobiles the 200 kilometers to Bandung to be close to military headquarters. As secretary to the director of the Governor General's Cabinet, I rode in one of the automobiles. Alette's Bandung family put up a bed for me in her room. Bed space in Bandung was hard to find. The town was bursting with military units who had retreated and had to be billeted, and with women and children evacuated from the outer islands.

Families were agonizing over what to do. A mass evacuation of the Dutch from Java was impossible. Where would they go? The Netherlands was occupied by Germany. Even if another country would welcome thousands upon thousands of evacuees, how would they be evacuated without ships to transport them? The only hope was that Java could be held.

When we said good-bye on February 21, Antoinette and I were optimistic. Perhaps Java could be held. Wasn't this what Father and other military men were planning for in Bandung?

Then, on February 28, 1942, the Japanese began landing on Java. No one could stop them.

On March 1, the Japanese forces occupied the airfield close to Bandung.

On March 5, Batavia surrendered.

Alette and I were in our room discussing what would happen now to Antoinette, stuck in Batavia with the Japanese, when someone rang the door bell. And there she was, wearing an enormous green military helmet and a plastic, green-and-brown raincoat over a filthy, muddy white overall. Her face was spattered with mud.

"Antoinette!" cried Alette. "How did you get here?"

"I drove in a convoy of new Chevrolet trucks that we wanted to keep out of Japanese hands."

"Why aren't you wearing your VAC uniform?" I asked.

"They were afraid of Japanese reprisals against VAC women. The corps was officially disbanded."

"I was let go, too," I threw in. "The boss didn't want me connected with him when the Japanese arrived. He thinks he might be taken prisoner. I was paid three months salary. And I have to tell you that Father called this morning and Java will capitulate in a few days."

"Come on, not so soon." Antoinette said. "I was counting on Bandung holding out for a while, at least. That's why I was so pleased about the opportunity to drive that truck here. I could see myself doing something useful here."

"You can do something useful in Australia. Father has arranged for the three of us to leave on a ship that's waiting for military and civilian evacuees. She's lying in Wijnkoop Bay on the south coast. I've been trying to reach you ever since Father called this morning to tell you to somehow come here. Thank goodness you are here. Father will send a military car for us at midnight."

"Isn't he coming with us?" Antoinette asked.

"No, he is going to fight with the guerrillas."

"I thought you just said Java was going to capitulate."

"Yes, but, if I understood it correctly, bands of ours will dig themselves in, in the mountains, and tie up Japanese troops. That will give the Allies time to organize and win the Indies back . . . Father said he would try to come by to say good-bye to us, but we shouldn't count on it. He may be tied up at headquarters."

"He probably added 'Duty comes before the girl,'" said Antoinette and when she saw me nod in agreement, a thin smile crossed her tired face.

"If we are going to leave tonight, we'd better start packing," I suggested. "Father said only one small rucksack each."

"I have nothing to pack," said Antoinette. "Can I borrow some clothes from you, Alette. We're the same size."

Alette decided to keep on her khaki uniform. Antoinette and I would travel in the outfits we had worn hiking on the volcanoes of Java, khaki shorts and shirts with button-flap pockets. Antoinette and Alette would wear comfortable sneakers. I happened to have my trail boots with me. Those light, hobnailed, leather boots had large canvas side-inserts so water could flow out after wading through rivers. We might have to walk partway to the coast.

We deliberated at length about what should go in the rucksacks, packed them, had dinner with the family, and waited for Father. But when the car came at midnight to pick us up, he still hadn't come. We had carried our rucksacks to the car and were returning to say good-bye to the family when a second car drove up ahead of ours and came to a squeaky stop. A tall, thin figure in green uniform jumped out and strode toward us.

"Who is this?" whispered Antoinette, and then, recognizing him she cried, "Father, Father!" and fell in his arms sobbing. "Oh, I'm so glad I can see you before leaving. I just hated to go without giving you a big hug."

Father patted her back. "It's all right, darling, I'm going with you. Get in the car quickly. Japanese troops are infiltrating on all sides, and the road to Wijnkoop Bay may not be clear much longer."

He transferred a brown sack marked "Preanger Hotel," and a tommy gun to the front seat next to the driver of the car. "You three sit in the back."

"Why are you going with us?" I asked.

"I'll tell you later. Let's be off now."

"What about Mother. Are we just going to leave her behind?" asked Alette.

Since the fall of Tarakan, none of us had ever added any "ifs" in our talks about Mother: "*if* she's still alive," "*if* she hasn't been executed,"—and we never would in the years to come. It was as though by not voicing the "ifs," even to ourselves, we could cause the "ifs" to go away.

"There is nothing we can do for her by staying in a Japanese-occupied country. I'm hoping that, once we are in the free world, the International Red Cross can arrange to have Mother and other Red Cross nurses in Tarakan released. They should never have been imprisoned. It's against the international conventions."

The car drove off into the dark. Father told us that the plans for guerrilla warfare had fallen through. It would only have led to needless manslaughter. The military chief-of-staff talked to Father earlier that evening, offering him a place on a plane to Australia. One of the last ones was leaving that night. He chose to go with us on the ship.

During the long, spooky trip, he kept the tommy gun's nozzle rested on the rolled-down window, but we didn't run into Japanese, only men with clipped English voices or thick, broad Australian accents. From lorries looming in the dark, they asked us where we were from and where we were going. Father couldn't very well say that we were from Bandung, and were heading south to catch a ship to take us away from Java because we had lost the war, when these troops were on their way to Bandung to help win the war. Father said he had business to take care of. One Aussie came off his lorry perch, looked inside the car and, seeing us girls in the back, said, "And you taking these three cute dishes along?"

We kept meeting columns of lorries, bulky 75 mms, and supply cars and tanks that took up most of the road. Men with caps, men with berets, men with big felt hats, one edge turned up, and men with helmets made hopeful remarks in cheerful, laughing voices. They were all heading toward Bandung, the last bulwark that we knew was already lost.

The sun was shining over the Indian Ocean when our car reached the bay, its blue water surrounded by green, jungle-covered hills. Big white breakers crashed on jagged, freakish looking coral reefs. Our driver helped us get our rucksacks out of the car and immediately turned back to Bandung. Father, my sisters, and I settled on the beach under a coconut palm, near another small group of evacuees. In the bay a sleek white ship with an orange smokestack was riding at anchor, the *Poelau Bras*, a 10,000-ton Dutch freighter of the Nederland Steamship Company, our ship.

"She should take 12 hours to get out of range of Japanese reconnaissance planes, and the bombers those planes will alert," said Father. "I don't think there are any submarines here to sink the ship."

"When are we going aboard?" I asked. "Why don't they send a sloop?"

"I guess the captain is waiting for more people to arrive. He will send a sloop later. He will get his instructions from Bandung."

All day we waited under the coconut palm. We munched sandwiches from the paper bag marked "Preanger Hotel." We drank the sweetish liquid inside the coconuts. A local lad had picked them for us high in the palm tree and punched the holes at their tops so the liquid could drip right into our upturned mouths. We talked with several other men who had come down the mountain road: men of the Royal Netherlands Navy, men of the Royal Netherlands Indies Army, and civilians. Several of these were BPM personnel responsible for destroying oil installations, eager to grab what seemed the last chance to stay out of Japanese hands. The men all came voluntarily in their own or official cars and left those cars at the end of the road near the seashore. (In later years I've often wondered whether the drivers of those cars took the keys with them on the ship or whether some turned to local men who had come to watch this exodus of whites, maybe men who couldn't even afford their own oxcarts, and said to them, "Here is the key, you can have that car.")

Finally, in the late afternoon, a sloop was launched and boarding began. I never knew how many people eventually packed on the ship. She had a crew of around 80. Estimates for the number of evacuees range from 170 to 250. Some were already on board when we arrived.

In the evening of March 6, 1942, the *Poelau Bras* lifted anchor and began sailing toward Australia.

Chapter Two

Shipwreck

So it happened that on March 7, 1942, I stood looking out over the Indian Ocean from the railing of the *Poelau Bras*, which was packed with evacuees from the Dutch East Indies hoping to make it to Australia. We soon should be out of danger—far enough from Java so that Japanese bombers stationed there could not attack the ship.

Next to me were Antoinette and Alette. We didn't speak. No other ships were in sight. The coast of Java had disappeared during the night.

I looked for Father close by, and saw him talking to a general. The deck of the freighter was a palette of white and green—the green of Army uniforms and the white of Navy uniforms and civilian men's tropical suits. Only a small portion of the evacuees were civilians, men on some mission or other. A few men brought their wives. Almost all were Dutch, but the night before I had noticed two American war correspondents with several cameras around their necks.

I started to think about the kind of war work we girls might be doing in Australia. I knew Antoinette had visions of driving trucks again in some Army Women's Corps, as she had done on Java. Just yesterday Alette had remarked that, of course, she had to go to school, she was only 16, but she knew all about telephone switchboards. Perhaps she could do something with that in Australia. "Anything I can do to get the Japanese out of the Dutch East Indies and get Mother back, I'll do."

It would have to be secretarial work for me. In Batavia I had had an interesting job. The next job might not be so interesting. Anyway, I knew I couldn't be choosy in the middle of a war. And I'd be going to a university in Holland when the Germans were ousted from there. Meanwhile, we were lucky to have space on this evacuation ship. I engrossed myself in these practical matters, trying not to worry about our mother.

I turned to my sisters. "This haze is good, we'll be less visible to enemy aircraft."

"I just heard someone say we are already 160 nautical miles Java," said Antoinette.

"We may make it, then," said Alette, and she straightened the collar of her khaki Orange Youth dress as if she were already sprucing up to walk off the gangplank in Australia.

She peered across the deck. "It looks like something is being served. It looks like lemonade. I'll go get us some."

She walked off, leaving her lifebelt on the deck.

"Take your lifebelt with you," Antoinette called after her. "We aren't out of danger yet."

Alette picked up the bulky grey lifebelt and wended her way past the clusters of men standing on the deck or sitting on coils of rope or on the tarp-covered hatch. I watched her side-step a mattress on which a naval officer's wife was changing her baby's diaper. The mother still wore the housecoat she had been wearing when her husband picked her up at the maternity ward of the hospital.

Alette returned with three glasses on a small tray in her right hand. In her left hand she held the lifebelt, which bumped against her leg with each step.

"We're not going to Australia," she said, excitedly. "We're going to Ceylon."

"But why?" I asked.

"Apparently the captain received orders from Java. The military people on board have to report to Ceylon. There's some kind of Allied Command there."

"But we packed winter clothes for Australia," I wailed. "We'll need tropical clothes in Ceylon."

"What does it matter?" retorted Antoinette. "We keep the winter clothes for after the war, when we go back to Holland, and we have new clothes made in Ceylon. They must have Chinese or Indian tailors there. You have the money Father gave us. As long as we get away."

I looked at my watch. "We are supposed to be out of reach of Japanese planes by eleven," I said. "It's almost eleven."

Moments later, a piercing blast of the ship's whistle split my ears.

I looked at the sky. Three specks were coming in our direction. "Oh God, they've spotted us . . . Why?" I moaned inwardly. "The sea is so immense, and we are so small. We are almost within reach of safety. Please, God, make them go back, make them turn around, please make them go back."

Army men ran to machine guns positioned at the railings. Everyone else on deck began to run. Father, carrying his lifebelt and wearing his helmet, ran toward my sisters and me. "Follow me to our lifeboat station," he shouted, "and bring your lifebelts."

He led us up a flight of stairs to a higher deck. Several people were running down the same flight of stairs. The ship's whistle continued to sound piercing, spine-tingling blasts. But it was silent when the four of us reached station number 2.

"Eleven blasts," cried Father. "General quarters. We aren't going to wait for the planes on this deck. We must take cover!"

The three specks had now become planes, and I saw that three more were coming toward us from another direction, and from yet another direction came three more. Nine planes! Nine against our ship. I noticed the captain had started a zigzagging course. Perhaps to dodge the bombs?

I saw our rucksacks lying near the railing where our lifeboat station was. That morning, at the lifeboat drill, my sisters and I had put the packs there. On top lay the military helmets Father had given us before we left Bandung.

"Pick up your helmets," he said and, with us following closely behind, he ran up the stairs to the officers' quarters on the deck above.

We stood in a mahogany-paneled corridor with several other passengers wearing Navy white or Army greens. I fooled with the helmet. Antoinette helped me to fasten the buckle of the leather band. I slipped into my lifebelt, covered with sturdy grey material. The two pillowy front panels had to be tied together with strings made of the same grey material.

"Let me see whether you fastened yours properly," said Father. He didn't like the bows I made in the strings, and undid them to make knots instead. "We don't want those strings to come undone."

"I bet you made proper square knots," I said, and for the first time that day I saw him smile. How tired he looked, and how thin he was. Always a strong, athletic type, he now looked almost fragile. Maybe it was because his green shorts were too big. His helmet certainly was. I could barely see his greying brows and green-blue eyes. I suddenly felt a great annoyance with some military outfitter on Java, who couldn't be bothered to take the trouble to find Father a helmet of the proper size. He checked the ties on my sisters' lifebelts too.

Judging by the sound, the planes were now very close. Volleys rattled from our machine guns.

A deep shattering roar ended in a whine. A plane was diving over the ship. I expected to hear an explosion. The plane came out of its dive with another roar, and only then did I hear the bomb explode. The ship shook, lurched, and shuddered. "A hit," I thought. "The ship has been hit, and I'm still alive. I'm still standing here pressed against the wooden wall."

The explosion had been in the stern. One of the men in the corridor said, "Dear Jesus," and crossed himself. Father threw one arm around my shoulder and another one around Alette's, and looking hard at Antoinette, who stood at Alette's other side, said, "We have to be calm."

A second plane dived over the ship. I held my breath. Again there was the first deep, shattering roar ending in a whine, and then the second roar as the plane pulled up out of the dive.

I heard only a dull thud. The ship merely trembled.

"A near miss," said Father.

A third plane dived over the ship. It missed again.

I saw Antoinette feeling first in one and then in the other breast pocket of her shirt.

"What are you looking for?"

"A handkerchief."

"What for?"

"To put between my teeth during the bombing. That's what someone told me people in London do during the blitz. I think it's to protect your ear drums."

A young crew member squeezed past our group. He didn't look much older than Alette. He stopped and pulled a clean, folded handkerchief from his pants pocket and handed it to Antoinette.

"Here, use mine. And what about you?" he asked Alette.

"I don't have a handkerchief either."

"I'll take care of you." He left and came back with a long strip of toilet paper in his hand. It was the coarse kind that feels like crinkly butcher paper.

He gave the strip to Alette. "It won't taste so hot, but you will all have something to bite on when the next bombs hit." Then he was gone.

Alette and I divided the strip of paper and folded it into tight little wads for Father and ourselves. I had mine between my teeth until it became so soggy that I almost choked on it and threw it away.

A second wave of planes roared near. Again there were three, diving down one after the other, in a roar followed by a whine, then pulling up in another roar. And three more. And three more. Some attacks ended in explosions, in the din of falling debris, shouted commands, and cries and screams of people who must have become trapped or wounded.

After the last plane left an eerie silence followed.

"The dirty swine, they hit the engine room!" I heard a young voice shout. Now I realized why it was so quiet. The engines had stopped. We would be a sitting duck for the attacking planes.

"Maybe the damage can be repaired and we can still make it to Ceylon," Father said. Then he added, his voice barely audible, "I hope I did all right in letting you girls go on this ship. If something happens to you, I'll never forgive myself. I have to bring you back to Mother."

And where was that? I wondered.

I had no time to make a guess. A man outside the corridor shouted, "To the lifeboats, everyone to the lifeboats," and all of us standing inside ran down the stairs to the deck to scatter to one of the eight assigned lifeboat stations.

Bodies and piles of wreckage were everywhere. The stern was ablaze. Figures in white scurried around with hoses and buckets of what I thought must be sand. Searing, hissing flames were spreading.

I could feel the heat of the flames on my face and hands. What if I can't get off the ship? The flames may blow this way any moment. I'll be roasted alive. Where is our lifeboat? It was supposed to be lowered from the

15

sloop deck above. That's what we were told during lifeboat drill. "Stand here near the railing and your boat will be lowered so you can get in."

I looked up and saw the grey-painted bottom of the boat still hanging motionless above me.

We were in a group of some 20 people, all of us waiting for the boat to come down. The flames were getting closer. The heat was becoming more intense.

I heard a pistol shot and near me someone said, "I guess he shot himself. Maybe he's better off. We're an awfully long way from the coast."

Yes, I thought, we are a long way from the coast, 160 sea miles. And only three lifeboats intact, I just heard. Three lifeboats for all the people on the ship. But will any of us be able to get off the ship before the flames spread, before the ship starts to sink, as she surely will?

I looked at my watch. It was 11:16. The alarm had sounded at 11:02, only 14 minutes ago. . .

"Why in the hell don't they lower the boat?" a man near me said. The boat above us was still motionless.

"Let's go to the sloop deck and bring the boat down ourselves."

"We don't know how."

"I'm sure we can figure it out."

"We're supposed to stay here."

"Wait! Here it comes. They're lowering it!"

But another plane came bearing down on the *Poelau Bras*, and the boat stopped before it reached our deck. Everyone near lifeboat station 2 hit the planks. I saw no one at the machine guns. Perhaps the gunners were dead.

I lay on my stomach. From under my helmet I surveyed those around me. Some were rolled up into balls. Others were stretched out like I was. One man calmly lay on his back, as if he were sunbathing at the beach. Wasn't he afraid of something falling on his face?

My muscles tightened. The plane roared down. Through the split between my helmet and my arms I saw silver wings and a fiery red disk underneath. There it was, the Rising Sun of Japan. I had only seen that red disk on a white flag flying in Batavia as a mark of respect for visiting Japanese officials, all those politely bowing and hissing gentlemen who had come to ask for more oil deliveries from the Netherlands East Indies gov-

16

ernment. Now the red sun shone on a plane manned by a Japanese pilot determined to sink our ship.

Banggg. The ship shuddered. Another hit. A second plane roared down, and a third. As the second and third planes left, the ship merely quivered. I heard only thuds on port.

Near misses again, I thought. They ought to run out of bombs soon. I scrambled up.

"Look at the bridge!" The bridge was hit. Wood and metal were crumpling. The bridge collapsed with a terrifying crash. From the bowels of the ship came a strange, hissing sound.

"Do you hear that noise?" I asked Father.

"Yes, the ship is taking on water. She will be sinking soon. We must get into the lifeboat."

The lifeboat still hung suspended between the sloop deck and our deck. I saw it move. Finally, it hung level with our deck.

People formed into an orderly line. No one pushed. The four of us were at the end. Why weren't we girls going into the lifeboat first? That's what you read in books, women have priority in lifeboats. But bombs were falling. Fires were spreading. Water was rushing into the ship. Was there time to think about shipwreck etiquette? The men in front may not even have known women were in the back. My sisters and I, dressed in military khaki, hair hidden by big green helmets, did not instantly advertise, "Women."

A ship's officer ran by and shouted, "No luggage in the boats!" I picked up my rucksack near the railing and hurled it out of the way. Antoinette and Alette did the same.

One after another the men ahead of us climbed over the railing into the swaying boat hanging above the sea. A burly, tow-headed sailor who had come down in the boat from the sloop deck pushed each one in and, as soon as the man was seated, rumbled, "Next one!"

"Next one!"

"Next one!"

Only a few people were left ahead of me when another plane appeared. No one went down on the deck this time. The ship obviously wouldn't last much longer. We had to get into the lifeboat.

Tat-tat-tat-tat-tat. Bullets splattered the deck. This pilot is machine-gunning us! Why would he do that? The ship is a goner. Isn't that enough?

Ahead of me a man in the line slumped silently sideways on the deck. He must have been hit. His eyes were open, and he had a smile on his lips. A pool of blood welled up under his body.

I looked at Father and my sisters. They were all right.

"Next one!" the sailor shouted.

"Go, Alette," said Father. She hesitated, crouched on the railing, holding onto an upright pole. I saw why. The lifeboat was sinking away. The men on the sloop deck were launching the boat.

"Wait a minute, there are more people who have to get in," the tow-headed sailor yelled. The men on the sloop deck didn't hear, or they didn't want to hear. They, too, wanted to get off the ship.

The lifeboat continued to sink slowly toward the sea.

"Jump!" the sailor shouted up to Alette, "I'll catch you!"

He stood up straight in the boat. Figures around him were bent over, heads between knees, all prepared for the next strafing plane.

Alette jumped and landed in the sailor's upstretched arms. He swung her onto an empty spot on the thwart next to him and caught Antoinette next. Now it was my turn.

I climbed on the railing, hung onto the pole and looked down. I could hardly hear the sailor's "Next one." Under the boat glimmered the sea. I saw that my sisters sat doubled up. Alette looked up at me and screamed, "Hurry, you can do it!" Behind me Father urged, "Come on, jump."

I saw another plane heading toward the ship, and I plummeted down into a mass of people. I felt strong arms around me. They lifted me like a package over several bodies and deposited me next to a haggard-looking man who dully said, "Congratulations."

Then Father jumped and sat close to me. The two girls were at the other end. The lifeboat had smacked down onto the water.

Someone cut the fall ropes with a knife. I felt relieved. Now the lifeboat would be able to move away from the sinking ship. Men were already pulling oars from under the thwarts and fumbling to put them in the locks.

Suddenly water rushed over my head. Water crushed me. Water strangled me. I am drowning, I thought. Before me, I saw a page of a green-bound book I read at my *gymnasium* in The Hague in an English class. It told the story of the sinking of the *Lusitania*. I am being sucked down with the sinking ship just like the woman in that story. I am drowning. I am going down with the ship. I am going to die. And I am not scared. I always thought I would be scared to die.

Suddenly, the *Poelau Bras* towered above me. The sky was as murky as when I last saw it.

"What happened?"

"A bomb exploded in the water next to us," said Father. Water dripped from his helmet. His cotton uniform clung to his wiry, muscular body. "We must get out of this boat, it is full of water."

"Antoinette, Alette, get out of the boat! Swim away as fast as you can!"

He and I clambered out of the boat. Several men also slid over the edge into the sea. Some had already been thrown overboard by the deluge of water.

Just as I started to swim, I passed a man I had talked with during breakfast. He had poured milk into my bowl of oatmeal. He was floating in his lifebelt on his back. His eyes were open, dull and still.

I couldn't swim in my hiking boots. I had anticipated a walk, perhaps a trek through the jungle to the coast. Now I lay on my back in my lifebelt in the sea and pulled off my boots. On the deck I had already loosened the laces. I also peeled off my knee socks and sent them after the boots. I had no idea how foolish it was to take off the boots and socks. They drifted away with the swell.

The swell surprised me. Surely there hadn't been a swell when I was standing at the railing before the planes came.

I turned over and breast-stroked away from the ship. I swam for a few minutes and turned on my back again to look for Father and my sisters. I saw none of them. No one at all was nearby.

Another plane dived down. I saw a bomb cut through the air. Strange, to actually see a bomb fall. It was grey and had little wings on its tail. The bomb came down at an angle. I saw it hit the ship and burst into yet more smoke and fire and flying debris.

Tat-tat-tat-tat-tat. The planes were still machine-gunning. One headed straight toward me. I turned forward again and tried to dive under the water, but my lifebelt wouldn't let me, and my helmet was in the way. So I kept swimming. The plane swooped down so close I could see the pilot's face. His skin was indeed yellow, and he had narrow, squinted eyes. He was Japanese all right. The only other Japanese I had ever seen were the visiting officials in Batavia who had played at the same golf links as Antoinette and

I. And I had talked to a Japanese man once in a camera shop in Tarakan. A spy, Father had said later. Now a Japanese pilot was emptying his machine gun at me. Bullets hit the water. Around me little fountains spurted up into the air.

The plane pulled away in a flash of silver wings and I was left with an afterimage of the odious red disk of the rising sun. Lying on my back again, I watched the *Poelau Bras*. She was leaning heavily toward the stern. On deck people were walking in the opposite direction, pushing their way "uphill." Some jumped from the deck into the sea. Some waved a white sheet, but the planes went right on strafing them.

Finally the planes left. And slowly, majestically, the *Poelau Bras* slipped underwater, her battered bow pointing toward the sky. The water churned, foamed, sent forth a big jet. And the ship was gone.

I looked again at my watch. Amazing, it was still running. The time was 11:36. It had taken 34 minutes to sink the ship. (The planes hadn't come from Java, as we surmised, but from the Japanese aircraft carrier *Hiryu*.)

All through the bombing, and through our escape from the ship and my solitary swim, I watched, I saw, but I did not feel. On my back in the water, I counted, methodically, 11 people jumping overboard. I saw men touch the water, but did not imagine the impact on their bodies of this almost suicidal jump. And I felt no concern as to their fate.

I watched the people waving the white sheet, but it would be many years before I could cry for them—over my typewriter—finally feeling the agony of begging for mercy while the planes went right on machine-gunning.

I saw every detail of the ship's sinking, but had not a single flutter of feeling for the people on it who knew there was nothing to do but wait for the water to close over them.

The swell seemed to have grown. It now took longer to swim the crest. Every time I reached the highest point, I looked for Father and Antoinette and Alette. I could see other swimmers, but no one who looked like them. Maybe they were already in one of the three boats in the distance. I also saw a raft with people on it. I hoped they wouldn't be on the raft because on board ship I had overheard that the rafts would have no chance at all of reaching land.

I panicked. I must get to one of those boats. I pulled the strap of my

The Poelau Bras that sank in the Indian Ocean on March 7, 1942. (Photo courtesy Section Maritime History of the Navy, Department of Defense, The Hague)

helmet over my chin and tipped the helmet in the water. Now it would be easier to swim.

I probably swam for an hour. I lost all track of time, riding the swells of the Indian Ocean. When I was in a trough I saw nothing but water. When I was on a crest I saw the boats. I tried to reach the closest one, but people were rowing the boat, and it moved away as quickly as I could swim. I felt seasick, perhaps from the sea water I swallowed or from the seesawing motion of the swell. I wanted to do nothing, to just float on my belt, but I knew I had to swim. If I didn't get into the lifeboat. . .

The lifebelt was slowing me down, but I didn't dare take it off. Besides, the knots Father had tied so carefully when we stood in the corridor of the *Poelau Bras* were impossible to untie now that they were wet.

Up on a swell again I saw that I was gaining on the boat. The people had stopped rowing and were trying to put up the mast. Now I really had to swim fast. If the lifeboat set sail, I'd never be able to catch up with it.

Finally, my hands were around the lifeline looped on the outside of the boat. Now that I had reached it, I couldn't think of what to do next. In the boat men were moving about, shouting to each other. The rope of the lifeline felt good in my hands. The grey wood of the boat gave me a sense of security. I really didn't want to do anything but feel that rope and look at the grey wood. Perhaps I should raise an arm and tell someone I'm here?

I don't know how long I hung onto the lifeline before I noticed a man looking at me. "You want to get in, I guess."

I was too numb to say anything, and merely nodded my head.

The man turned around and said, "Somebody wants to get in. It's a woman." I heard voices raised in anger.

"We can't have any more people in the boat. We are overloaded already."

"Try to save one more, we'll perish."

They didn't want me in the boat . . .?

The man looked down at me again. Another man appeared next to him. They lowered their arms. I put my hands in theirs. They pulled me into the boat.

"Sit down here," one of the men said. "That one is dead, do you mind?" A head was lying near my feet. Dark curly hair. Eyes closed. Army uniform. I hadn't seen him on the ship.

A huge wave of seasickness came over me. I bent over the edge of the boat and threw up. Someone laid a hand on my forehead, just as Mother did when I was little. Mother. Where was my mother? Oh yes, I remembered, she was a prisoner of the Japanese. But Father? Where was Father.

"Helen! Helen!"

Father's voice! I looked up and saw him at the other end of the crowded boat. I waved joyously and threw up again.

When I seemed to be completely empty inside, I crawled to him, helped by a lift here and a push there, stumbling over knees and feet. He squeezed my hand. Through the haze of continuing nausea I searched the faces around me for my sisters.

"Where are the other two?"

"I don't know. I thought they followed us when you and I went out of the lifeboat. I looked for them in the water, but they weren't there. I had hoped they would be in this boat."

"Which boat is this. Is this our number 2?"

"No, number 2 is over there." Father pointed to another sloop jammed with people. That boat had its sails up already and was moving away from the scene of the wreck.

"Maybe the girls are still in the boat. Maybe they never got out when you and I did," I suggested.

"If only you're right. But why don't I see them? No one in that boat is wearing a helmet any more. Without a helmet I should be able to spot Alette's blond hair." He shaded his eyes and looked again at the other boat.

I had to throw up again, and this time it was Father who put his hand on my forehead.

As I hung my head over the edge of the boat, I heard voices raised behind me. "The girl was positively the last one. We cannot pick up any more!"

"But we can't let him drown."

"He can go on the raft; it hasn't left yet."

"Come on, the raft doesn't have a chance. We all know that. We're much too far from the coast."

"Let's take him anyway."

"No, we'll never make it to land if we do. This tub is full of holes."

"What holes?"

"I don't know, machine-gun holes, I guess. We're taking water like a sieve." (By the next day the holes would shut with the heat.)

The argument continued. I sat up again and heard a calm voice saying we should pick up this man.

Another voice agreed. When the swimmer was pulled in, I saw he was William McDougall, one of the two American war correspondents.

"We have to take care now of the burial," the same voice said. It belonged to a man who sat on the stern bench next to the tiller and later introduced himself as the third officer of the *Poelau Bras*. He was in charge of this lifeboat.

Men pulled the corpse from under the thwarts, emptied his pockets, ripped off his uniform insignia, and gave the mementos to the skipper. Taking a grip on the dead man's feet and armpits, two men threw him overboard. "One, two, three in the name of the Lord." Men who still had helmets on took them off. One man didn't.

"For Christ's sake, can't you show respect for the dead?" yelled a freckled-faced sailor with a mop of red, curly hair. He reached over and yanked the helmet off the other man's head.

"Let's observe a minute of silence," said the skipper.

It became very still in the boat.

The men had another try at hoisting the mast—a mast about eight meters tall, almost as long as the boat. This time the mast stayed up. They hoisted the little foresail and the mainsail, a rectangle of canvas that swung out over the boat on a heavy boom.

"Now we can start sailing toward land," said the skipper. "Let me show you where we are and where we are going." He held up a chart I had already seen him studying while others were fussing with the mast and the sails, and pointed out where we were.

"We also have a compass on board, and I have my sextant. We will be sailing a northeastward course. This will land us on Sumatra."

"You're crazy!" shouted the red-haired sailor. "The Japs are there!" He was echoed by several others. The skipper raised his voice.

"Let me finish, please. The projected course is the best one to sail in view of prevailing currents and winds. We can't sail in the opposite direction to Australia, much as we'd like to. We'd never make it. Maybe the Japanese Army hasn't reached the stretch of Sumatra coast where we'll be landing. Escape may still be possible."

He hurried on, as if afraid of more interruptions. "One of the water tanks has been punctured and is empty. Water from the other tank will have to be rationed, and there won't be much for each. We are 25 in the boat—24 men and a woman—and a dog," and he pointed to the red-haired sailor. "Red brought Whiskey." A little black mongrel looked up from his spot on Red's knees and growled. The skipper went on.

"The only food aboard is hardtack, and I'm afraid there isn't much, so it will have to be rationed, too. If we're lucky the wind will hold and we'll reach land soon."

A chorus of voices asked, "How soon?" The skipper answered, "It could be just a couple of days."

The skipper sat at the tiller. A breeze blew our sails. Our boat began its voyage toward land. It was about four in the afternoon of March 7, 1942.

I sat close to Father. For a long time he kept looking at the other two boats, moving farther and farther away from us. There was no need to ask him what he was thinking.

Chapter Three

A Week in a Lifeboat

Water. Water to moisten my parched throat and wet my sunburned lips. It was our fourth day at sea.

"Coming up for our lady," said the man with the red, curly hair.

He was seated next to the skipper at the tiller, the undamaged water tank in front of him, and pulling a chain with a rusty tubular measure through the opening of the tank. The measure can't have been more than four centimeters in diameter and twelve centimeters across. We also used it as a cup.

I watched Red from where I was sitting on the gunwale near my father, huddled with two other men under a canvas stretched over the bow to protect against the spray. Already I had made a decision. I would not drink my ration in a few, greedy gulps, but would sip a little water from the cup, slowly swish it around in my mouth, and savor it as I swallowed. The noon ration was six hours away.

Red unhooked the cup from the chain and looked inside to make sure it was no more than half-filled; this was the ration issued three times a day, as decided upon after heated discussions. He passed the cup toward me. I watched my water moving from the hand of Mac, the American journalist, to the big, calloused hand of a *Poelau Bras* sailor, to the slim, brown hand of the ship's Javanese stoker, to the hand of someone I could not place, to the hand of a Dutch Navy officer.

Finally, the cup was in my hand. I had craved, longed, yearned for this water since the water ration the evening before, twelve hours ago. I drank the water as planned. I let my tongue play with the water in my mouth. I relished every taste.

After I had drained the last drop, I passed the cup back to Red, and soon everyone had a turn and could begin thinking about the next ration. This morning I was among the last to be served. That was the way Red's system worked. In the evening he started the measure moving clockwise around the oval of people sitting on both gunwales and then directed it to those who sat in the center of the boat on the thwarts, from bow to stern. At noon he passed the measure counterclockwise and down the thwarts, from stern to bow. And in the morning, as now, these thwart rows were first, and the people on the outer oval last.

We never sat on the same spot, but no one seemed alert or astute enough to beat the system by sitting close to wherever the slow and carefully watched procession of the water measure would start at any given rationing time.

As always, Red poured the last ration in a billy can and gave it to Whiskey. She was still on board despite cries of, "Throw her in the ocean!" "Why should I give up some of my water for a dog?" "She only takes up precious lifeboat space."

Red kept arguing that the dog had been the mascot of the *Poelau Bras*, and it would bring bad luck to the lifeboat if we did away with her. He kept Whiskey on his lap during most of the lifeboat voyage. She seemed happy there, but snarled at the rest of us. When it was Red's turn to lie on his back on the bottom of the boat, on a pallet made of six parallel oars, the mongrel lay curled up on his stomach.

On this ribbed "washboard bed," which wiggled every time someone shifted position, four of us could stretch our cramped muscles and perhaps catch some sleep. We slept for two-hour spells, according to a strict rotation schedule governed by one naval officer's alphabetized and memorized list of passengers.

"Anyone for hardtack?" asked Red.

A few said "Yes," but I muttered "No, thank you." Those round dog biscuits tasted of sawdust and sand and only made the thirst worse. Anything to minimize that terrible thirst . . . I knew another day of doldrums was ahead.

Doldrums, once only a word I'd learned in school. "To be in the doldrums" meant to be depressed. In Dutch *in de put zijn*. I remember my English teacher saying, "The expression derives from a belt of calms near the equator. To be becalmed for weeks, perhaps in the hottest sun, was one of the fears of ancient sailors, like the one in Coleridge's 'Rime of the Ancient Mariner.'"

Now I knew what doldrums meant. Sea as smooth as glass, and a large sail hanging limp between the staff and boom alongside the mast, providing nary a shadow. Doldrums meant a brassy sun that blistered the skin, cracked the lips, and made the wood of the lifeboat fiery hot to the touch. Doldrums meant 25 people sitting on the gunwales and the thwarts with knotted handkerchiefs or cut-off shirttails tied on their heads, and eyes closed against the glare of the sun, looking like chickens on a roost in the middle of a hot summer day. It meant even big, husky men leaning against the shoulder of a mate, looking helpless and vulnerable.

This is what Coleridge had to say, under the section, "The ship hath been suddenly becalmed."

> *Down dropt the breeze,*
> *the sails dropt down*
> *'Twas sad as sad could be;*
> *And we did speak only to break*
> *The silence of the sea!*
>
> *All in a hot and copper sky*
> *The bloody Sun, at noon,*
> *Right up above the mast did stand,*
> *No bigger than the Moon.*
> *Day after day, day after day,*
> *We stuck, nor breath nor motion;*
> *As idle as a painted ship,*
> *Upon a painted ocean.*

Water, water, every where,
And all the boards did shrink;
Water, water every where,
Nor any drop to drink.

In the lifeboat we were better off. We did have a few drops to drink. And at night the wind came up. First it was a gentle, soothing breeze. As the sails billowed and the boat started moving across the water toward land, spirits soared. We even sang, a special pleasure for me, since now no one told me I'd better not sing along because I couldn't carry a tune.

Mac introduced American favorites like, "My Old Kentucky Home," "Home, Home on the Range," which some of the Dutch already knew. Or we sang Dutch patriotic songs, such as the one about the Dutch flag flying atop sand dunes, and Dutch folksongs about frogs lying half-dead in a frozen canal or two hares sitting in a green, green turnip field.

Once we sang hymns, led by a man with a fine baritone voice. Even now, I can never hear "A Mighty Fortress Is Our God" without thinking of our puny lifeboat sailing over an immense ocean along a shimmering path of moonlight, and a group of tattered, shipwrecked souls pouring out their hopes in Luther's powerful hymn.

But soon the friendly breeze became a furious blast that tore right through our clothes, newly soaked by ocean spray, making us as cold during the night as we had been hot during the day. Silence returned to the boat.

The first evening in the boat each military man had torn the insignia off his uniform and put them out of sight. This was to ease the matter of discipline. I had helped Father remove from his shirt the gold badge with his silver major's star. He had another reason for removing his military gold. If the Japanese caught him, he didn't want to be identified as a Royal Netherlands East Indies Army officer. It wouldn't take the Japanese military long to find out he was an escaped hostage, and this would surely mean his death.

I don't know how exemplary the discipline in our boat was compared to similar lifeboat situations. The skipper was not an assertive man, but he was usually able to hold his own, backed up by the quiet, sensible types.

At night several of the men spelled the skipper at the tiller. My father was one of them. He wasn't a good sailor. When my sisters and I were children in Holland, Mother and he had taken us to lakes near The Hague for outings on a rented sailboat. There had always been much flapping of sails resulting from Father's unsuccessful tacking maneuvers, and we frequently had landed in the rushes.

Still, Father knew enough to keep the lifeboat sailing before the wind in the direction the skipper pointed out on the compass.

The fourth day went by as the previous days had, except that by now we had given up rowing. We had been rowing in 30-minute shifts—four persons to a thwart, two to each of the six oars. It had been suggested that I should be exempt from rowing, but I insisted. I could do my share equally. I also knew it was better to do something and be miserable than to just sit like a pudding in the boat and be miserable. But when a unanimous decision was reached—probably the only unanimous decision ever reached in that boat—that it was pointless to row a big cumbersome boat with big cumbersome oars in the sizzling heat when at night the wind would come up and push the boat, I certainly didn't object. The rowing had been hard work and the sun relentless.

The fourth day the sea again was mirror-smooth. The sun was searing. And our thirst was awful.

We had our water rations, and some men chewed on hardtack. Someone passed his comb so we could all tidy our hair. Men went over to the side to relieve themselves. I used a helmet like a bedpan and someone emptied it into the sea. Dehydration lessened the need for the helmet.

Neighbors quarreled over inches of space or the accidental digging of an elbow into a side. Words such as "shit" or "son-of-a-bitch" were tossed into the air, and often one man would say, "Mind your language, there's a lady present."

Then it was silent in the boat again. The sun was relentless. The thirst was terrible.

Talk about swimming had been going on since the second day. Was it wise? We had seen the triangular fins of sharks piercing the water. On the other hand, if no sharks were in sight, water would cool us down, provide an opportunity to stretch. Could we go in without swallowing salty sea water, which would make us more thirsty yet? Red told a story of a group of people shipwrecked earlier in the war who had drunk sea water and gone mad.

In the afternoon someone finally jumped out of the motionless boat to go for a swim. He breast-stroked around the boat with his head above water and his mouth firmly closed. Others followed suit. Some men, not trusting their strength after several days of fasting, cautiously lowered themselves into the sea and, with one arm hooked onto the lifeline, made circular, tension-loosening motions with their other arm and moved their legs like frogs or in scissor-like movements.

"What shall we do?" I asked Father.

"Why don't you go in, too? There don't appear to be sharks around. Stay close to the boat. We'll watch for sharks."

As I lowered myself from the rim, he called, "Keep the sea water out of your mouth!"

How utterly marvelous the water felt. I twisted and stretched every stiff and tired muscle, but I never let go of the lifeline and stayed in the water only a few minutes. When Father and someone else helped me get back into the boat, I had the extraordinary sense of coming home. I felt safe.

I didn't go in the water again. No one else went swimming again either. The temptation to drink from the sea was simply too great. Sitting in the boat with wet clothes was cooling only for a moment. The sun burned down hot as ever and dried our clothes all too quickly.

On the fourth night the moon and the stars disappeared. The sky became inky black. Lightning flashed. Thunder rolled. A curtain of rain raced toward us, poured over us, and soaked our clothes. I started to suck the rain from my sleeves, only to become furious with myself for having gone swimming that afternoon. The clothes tasted of salt. I pulled my hair over my face and sucked rain from my hair. Now there was no salt. Then I tilted my head back and let the rain fall directly into my open mouth.

Next to me Father held up his helmet. I heard the drops pelt inside. When the helmet was full, he gave it to me. "Here, have your fill."

Deliriously, I gulped half the rain water down and gave the helmet back to Father.

Meanwhile, some men had pulled up a folded tarp, unfolded it, and were holding it to catch the rain. Heads bent over the canvas slurping the rain filling the just-fashioned well.

"Let's first collect water for the water tank," a voice shouted. No one listened. The rain stopped as suddenly as it had begun.

In the wake of the rain came a small hurricane. The first squall almost capsized the boat. Men hastily reefed the mainsail and the little foresail. Incoming waves filled the boat with water. Some men put their lifebelts on.

"All hands bail," the skipper hollered into the wind. The boat bucked up and down on the waves as he hung on to the tiller.

We bailed with billy cans, with helmets, with our hands.

The storm abated. The boat was still full of water. For several more hours we bailed. When the boat was dry, the man with the fine baritone began singing. No one joined in. His deep voice trailed off over the vast black sea.

The stars came out. I felt so numb that I barely noticed.

The sails were hoisted. Again we moved toward land.

When morning finally came, I saw the contour of a mountain on the horizon. After a while nothing was left but the ocean that stretched as far as the eye could see.

"Was that a mirage?" I asked Father.

"Yes, it was."

The sun beat down. The thirst was getting worse and worse. Now in our fifth day at sea, minds started to crack.

One man waved a pistol as he chanted, "toodloo-toodloo toodloo-toodloo-toodloo" in a monotonous voice, ending this phrase with a modulated, "Give me water, or I'll shoot." Each time he gave more emphasis to the word shoot, and when the word sounded really harsh and angry, the man next to him grabbed the pistol and dropped it into the sea. I was afraid the owner of the pistol would make a scene, but he merely went on chanting "toodloo-toodloo-toodloo-toodloo-toodloo," now omitting the threat of shooting. As he stared into space, he moved his head from side to side in time with his chant.

Another man wanted to throw all the lifebelts overboard. "I can't stand the sight of the bloomin' things! They make me think of the shipwreck and those blasted pilots." Someone talked with him, and he calmed down.

Yet another man, for no apparent reason, began to laugh, and his laughter, erupting in moments of great silence, had an eerie, upsetting ring.

The moments of silence were fewer now. Quarrels, griping, and complaints escalated. "If the voyage had lasted much longer," I wrote in my diary a few weeks later, "we would have *all* gone bananas."

31

How was it to spend seven days in a lifeboat as the only woman with 24 men? Except for such occasional niceties as, "Watch your language, there's a lady present," or my proffered exemption from rowing, the gender difference did not seem to matter. We were all shipwrecked human beings. We were all blistered by the sun, chilled by the wind, racked with hunger and thirst. Apart from the few sing-songs in the early evening and the memorable swimming party, we barely communicated with one another. We merely sat and waited to reach land.

Of some men in the boat I remember only parts: a voice that spoke softly or in anger, a hand that passed the water cup or bailed, unwashed feet placed next to my face as I took my turn lying on the oars. Of a man, named Piet, I remember mostly the wound on his leg.

Shortly after I was pulled into the lifeboat someone had asked me to dress the wound of an injured man. Now the difference in gender was significant: traditional "woman's work" went automatically to me. At the time, I thought this was natural. Now I think some of the men would have made better nurses.

The man called Piet pulled off his shoe and sock and showed me a raw flesh wound on his calf. Through the haze of nausea and shock, instructions from a first aid course Antoinette and I had taken on Tarakan came back to me. Excessive bleeding, turn off flow of blood . . . When leg bleeds, make a tourniquet on the thigh . . . Use a handkerchief and a stick of wood or pencil. A handkerchief, I thought, I don't have one.

"Anyone have a handkerchief?"

I received two.

Then I was handed a fountain pen. "Here, use this. There's no ink in it."

I must hurry, I told myself, the leg is still bleeding badly. I folded the handkerchief diagonally, pushed up the white crumpled material of Piet's shorts, and laid the handkerchief around the thigh, twisting the cloth tightly with the fountain pen. After a few minutes I released the tourniquet, then tightened it, and released it again as I remembered doing on a perfectly healthy practice leg on Tarakan. Much to my surprise, on this injured leg, the bleeding stopped.

Several men were watching me, giving advice.

"You can use the handkerchiefs for salt water compresses." "You need a bandage to wind around the leg." "Is there a first-aid kit on board?" "There doesn't seem to be."

I heard the tearing of cloth as someone ripped strips from the bottom of a shirt, and I was presented with a roll of it, the segments tied together with knots. I soaked the handkerchiefs with sea water, applied them to the wound, rolled the bandage around the leg, and repeated this every evening of the voyage. Piet spent most of the trip under the spray canvas over the bow.

Some faces remain in my memory, and in some cases I can put a personalitiy with a face. The skipper was blue-eyed and blond and only a year older than me. I wondered how he felt to be in charge of men twice his age who, before the shipwreck, had been above him in rank or social status.

The memory of Mac, the war correspondent, remains intact for me too. He often sat on the gunwale near the bow, his bare feet dangling above the water. He was a foreigner among us Dutch, a little island unto himself. He did not understand a word of our language, and several of the Dutch did not speak English. Mac liked to talk with Father, who spoke English fluently and could answer Mac's journalistic questions. They talked about the scorched-earth policy, whether it had been successful, about the defense of the Dutch East Indies, or the lack of it, and about what Sumatra would be like when we landed there.

If we talked about anything as a group, that was it. Sumatra was a huge island. Someone even knew the exact measurements: 1,700 kilometers long and 430 kilometers wide, "about 13 times as large as Holland." Would we run into the Japanese upon landing? Probably not. We were heading for an isolated coast with just a few tiny villages backed by jungle. One of our group had been in the area. "Nothing to find there for an occupying army."

What would the army do if it caught us?

Mac was sure we would all be interned. "Japan wants to create a Greater East Asia Coprosperity Sphere. Asia is to be for the Asians. The Japanese won't have any use for whites."

Father translated Mac's viewpoint into Dutch.

"Why would they do that? There are thousands and thousands of whites in the Dutch East Indies. They can't possibly intern us all," Red protested. "They'll let the whites go about their business, just as the Germans are doing with the Dutch in occupied Holland."

"Yes, they will need whites to keep the plantations going, and to restore the damage we did to factories, oil wells, and refineries," suggested someone else.

"What do you think the Japanese will do?" I asked Father.

"I don't know, but we are going to try to get away before we have time to find out, as soon as we have found Antoinette and Alette." If he ever contemplated the possibility that my sisters might not have made it to either of the other two lifeboats, or that they might have been killed by machine-gun fire and thrown overboard like the man in our boat, he didn't say so.

On the sixth day, we thought land must be near. We saw a seagull. The bird flew away and no land came into sight. The wind had gone down as usual.

We were hot. We were thirsty. No one spoke.

At one o'clock on our sixth night at sea, when we were sailing again at a good clip and I had fallen asleep sitting on one of the thwarts, Father shook me by the arm.

"We are near land."

It was a clear, starry night. Men reefed the sail. Someone stood on the bow sounding for depth with a weighted line. Beyond his silhouette I still saw nothing but the ocean. But from the direction we were heading came a strange new sound: the sound of surf beating against a shore. From the same direction came a heavy sweet smell.

Men hoisted the sails again, and we sailed toward the sounds and smells of Sumatra.

In the dawn I could make out a straight line on the horizon. The straight line became a bumpy line. The bumpy line turned into curving beaches sweeping down from hills covered with jungle, mentioned in the boat the previous day. Just perfect for hiding from the Japanese, I thought.

The skipper held up his chart and showed us that we were near Semangka Bay at the southernmost tip of Sumatra. "As you'll see, this bay opens into the Sunda Straits between Sumatra and Java. Straight ahead of us lies a small island called Tabuan, at the entrance to the bay. We'll land at Tabuan."

When the wind went down, Red issued an extra water ration, and we manned the oars. Around noon we threw the anchor just behind enormous breakers rolling out toward a deserted beach lined with coconut palms. I could see the coconuts clustered at the top, and our Javanese passenger promised to climb into the palms and get a nut for each of us.

"Someone has to swim ashore right away to tie the boat to a tree," the skipper said. "The anchor may not hold, and we don't want to be swept right back out to sea."

"I'll go," the Javanese volunteered.

With sure steady strokes, the dark lean man swam ashore, carrying one end of a line tied to our mast. I kept losing sight of him, but he reappeared with the breaking of each wave. Then he waded to the beach and fastened the other end of the line to a tree. I saw him walk around on the beach, gaze up at the coconut palms, and lie down on the sand. It looked as if he had fallen asleep immediately. No people appeared on the beach. That's good, I thought. The less our landing is publicized, the better.

In the boat we were getting ready to go ashore. Everyone would leave except Piet. Some men, looking at the heavy breakers, put their lifebelts on.

"Let's make sure we have no incriminating papers on us," warned Father, "and dispose of the military insignia and our weapons."

Out of the nooks and crannies of the boat came the insignia ripped off the first evening, and pistols and military helmets. Out of pockets came passports, driver's licenses, club membership cards. Anything that would serve as identification had to go. If we ran into the Japanese, we would be nobodies, shipwrecked without a past.

Reluctantly, I added my letter of reference written by the director of the Governor-General's Cabinet lauding my secretarial qualities. The official letterhead might interest the Japanese. I also gave up the pictures I had unglued from a photo album just before leaving Bandung for Wijnkoop Bay. Sea water had blurred the scenes anyway. But I kept the water-stained graduation certificate of my *gymnasium*. I couldn't bear to surrender this tangible proof that, not so long ago, in a normal world, I had actually passed exams in Latin and Greek and modern languages, and history, and math.

Father folded all the papers and weapons into the canvas we had used to catch water during the rain storm, tied a piece of rope around it, and dropped the bundle into the sea.

"Don't all leave the boat at once," the skipper said. "Some of us may want to hold onto the line, but safer to leave spaces in between."

For the last time the passengers of the boat were assigned turns. "We'll start with the N's," said the skipper. The naval officer who had memorized the list named the four people who would go first.

Some men indeed hung onto the connecting line but in the breakers they tumbled, and as I watched from the lifeboat they disappeared for a frighteningly long time before they resurfaced.

When Red swam ashore, Whiskey paddled next to him. Her little black head, with the one ear standing up and the other lying down, stayed close to the head with the carrot-colored hair. When Red reached the breakers, he grabbed Whiskey by the neck and held her in front of him. Swimming with just one arm, he crested the breakers and waded ashore.

"You'd better wear your lifebelt," said Father when it was our turn. "You aren't as strong as you used to be, and I think we should swim all the way rather than holding onto that line. It would be a disadvantage to be clinging to it when we go through the breakers."

"Fine," I said. But inside I was quaking at the thought of big breakers sucking me down, swinging me around in a vortex of water mixed with sand, shells, and pebbles, and then making me wonder whether I'd ever see the sky again. I had experienced such waves at a Bali beach. And I was trying not to remember all that water that swept over me when the bomb exploded next to the *Poelau Bras.*

Father sat on the gunwale of the boat and lowered himself into the water. He, too, must feel weak, I thought. The realization came almost as a surprise. To his children, Father had always been a man of strength and vigor. I followed him out of the boat, still wondering at the novelty of having to worry about *his* endurance.

With Father in the lead, I swam toward land. He looked back again and shouted, "Now swim as fast as you can and try to stay on top of the waves."

I stayed on top. After we rode smoothly in on the breakers, Father gave me one of his "well done" smiles, and together we swam a little further and waded onto the island of Tabuan.

The date was Friday, March 13, 1942.

Chapter Four

Meeting in the Jungle

For the second time in eight days, I watched a Javanese climb up the tall trunk of a coconut palm. The first time I had been sitting with my father, sisters, and a group of well-groomed men in crisp military uniforms or neat, newly laundered tropical suits on a beach on Java. The *Poelau Bras* was riding at anchor in the bay. I had watched the native boy without much interest. I was neither thirsty nor hungry.

Now I was sitting with my father on a beach of an island off Sumatra. The *Poelau Bras* was gone. Antoinette and Alette were no longer with us. The men around me were unshaven and wore dirty, rumpled, sunbleached clothes, still wet from their swim ashore. The inside of my mouth felt like a dried apricot. My tongue felt like sandpaper. I watched the climbing man with passion and noticed every detail.

He hugged the trunk with his arms and, planting his bare feet squarely against the trunk, took small steps upward, his knees bent outward. Then he pushed his arms up higher, took more steps, and so moved up the palm as gracefully and easily as a squirrel. When he reached the crown and the thick cluster of nuts, he picked one, held it in his hand, looked down to

The third lifeboat that landed near Krui with 54 passengers. (Photo courtesy Section Maritime History of the Navy, Department of Defense, The Hague)

where we were standing, and shouted, "Look out below, I'm going to throw it."

Everyone scurried out of the way. With a dull thud, the coconut plopped in the sand.

The stubborn lifeboat chivalry was still in force: the first nut was for me. One man had already found a sharply pointed stone to use as a kind of awl and another stone to use as a hammer. Using these, he punched two holes in the shell. He shook the nut gently so I could hear the liquid slosh, and then handed it to me.

Thinking of the six grueling days and nights at sea with only those minute water rations three times a day, I tipped my head back, held the nut high with both hands, and put one of the holes to my lips. I couldn't let myself realize how thirsty I was until I felt the sweet transparent coconut liquid trickle into my mouth, and keep on trickling, with the certain knowledge that if I wanted more than this one nut, I could ask for a second one. With fruit-bearing palms up and down the beach, there were enough nuts to go around more than once. Father and others were drinking now, too. The Javanese was still in the same tree, tossing coconuts onto the sand.

I thought about the meat inside the nut I held in my hands. How to open it? On Java, I had seen locals use razor-sharp *parang's*, wooden-handled curved knives, to slice off the outer rind of the nut and then cut, or tear off by hand, the next layer of shaggy husk, baring the hard kernel. The next step would be to whack the kernel against a rock or hit it with a stone or hammer to break it into two halves lined with shiny, white coconut meat.

Somehow the others had managed to open their nuts and were whittling off the meat with a pocket knife and gorging themselves. But Father stopped me from wondering how I would open mine. "The meat's too rich for our shriveled stomachs," he warned. "Better hold off now and start eating again with something like rice."

Meanwhile Red, with a coconut bulging under his shirt and a couple of rock tools in his pocket, had swum back to the lifeboat and Piet. I didn't see Red return to the beach. By then I was fast asleep, sprawled in the sand. In closing my eyes, I had given up thoughts of where the Japanese were and what they would do if they caught us. All that mattered as I sank into sleep was that we had not perished at sea. We were on land. We could drink as much as we wished. We could sleep with lots of space between us.

I woke to Father's gentle prodding. "I'm going for a reconnaissance. Want to come?"

I scrambled up. "What's the matter? The beach is moving."

"You haven't got your land legs yet. It may take some time before we lose the sensation of being in the boat."

The two of us started to walk. Beyond the strip of beach were bushes and trees and a little path that indicated the island was inhabited. I took deep breaths, filling my lungs with air. My toes dug into earth. I had survived the shipwreck and the lifeboat. I was on land—land that moved up and down, but solid land.

"The people here may have had news about the other boats," said Father. "You know how fast news travels in these areas."

39

He was referring to the *kabar angin*, the local population's astonishing "wind news." In some of the remote outer districts of the Dutch East Indies, people had neither telephones nor radios, but they seemed to pluck news out of the air with their hands, if not out of their sonorous, far-carrying drums.

Suddenly I realized we were not alone. From the brush to our right dark eyes peered at us.

"Look, there *are* people."

Father spoke to them in Malay, the lingua franca among the many different peoples of the Dutch colony, but they didn't answer.

"They must think we are ghosts," I said. "They probably see few white people on the island, let alone types who look like scarecrows, like us."

Father spoke again to the figures in the bushes, and a wrinkled man, wearing a purple sarong, a white cotton jacket buttoned all the way up the front, and a white fez ambled toward us. So the man was a *hajji*, a Muslim who had made a pilgrimage to Mecca. In his village he would be a man of prestige.

The hajji asked the obvious question, "Where do you come from?"

Father explained our presence on Tabuan, and told him that 23 men on the beach would very much appreciate cooked rice, as would we.

The hajji said he was sorry that Allah had put evil in our path. His village was poor, but he could always spare rice. He sent a little boy, squatting some distance away, to ask his mother for it.

While waiting for the boy to come back, Father and I and the hajji squatted on the trail and talked. We learned that the Japanese had already established themselves at the far end of Semangka Bay, in a town called Kota Agung, on Sumatra's mainland, and several hours sailing from Tabuan.

"We don't want to go to Kota Agung," Father said. "Will we meet the Japanese if we go in the other direction? If we are taken to the nearest Sumatra beach and then walk around the Vlakke Hoek and north up the Sumatra coast. . .?"

"No, you won't. The Japanese are in Krui, but that's still a long, long way from Vlakke Hoek."

"And are there villages north of Vlakke Hoek?"

"Yes, there are, small ones, but they get bigger as you get closer to Krui."

I knew why Father asked. In the lifeboat he had told me about a possible escape route. We would have a man from one of those villages take us in a native sailing craft to the Mentawei Islands, a string of islands in the Indian Ocean off the Sumatra coast. But first, of course, we would find Antoinette and Alette.

"I saw on a map in our lifeboat that there is a lighthouse at Vlakke Hoek. It may have news about the two other lifeboats from the *Poelau Bras*. I think the other two boats will have landed farther north than we. My two other children are in one of those boats. So I want to go to the lighthouse."

The hajji nodded his head, and in silence we waited until the boy returned.

In one hand he held the handle of a large, black-smoked, round-bellied iron pot filled with white boiled rice. In the other, he had a spoon and a cracked china cup filled with salt crystals. Father asked the hajji to come with us and, with the small boy walking behind, carelessly swinging the pot of precious food, we rejoined the others at the beach.

"You can divide the food," said Red, assigning me another conventional female role, now as server. "Use these for plates," he said, handing me a few banana leaves he had plucked from a tree. "Sorry, no bananas on the tree."

Others helped me tear, native fashion, horizontal strips to the center vein of the big leaves. I lined these strips up on the sand and spooned out equal blobs of rice, sprinkling crystals of salt on each of them. Little did I know that equally dividing—taking away a smidgen here, adding a smidgen there—would be a part of my life for the next three-and-a-half years.

I put a portion aside for wounded Piet out there beyond the breakers. One of the men on the beach folded a strip of banana leaf around it, using a small twig as a pin. "I'll eat when I come back," he said, and set off with the package to the lifeboat.

I ate my portion of the rice, and the worst of the hunger pains left me.

When everyone had scraped the last grain of rice from his banana leaf with his fingers, or licked it with his tongue, it was time to plan the future. We couldn't stay on Tabuan. The population would be unable to feed the 25 of us. Besides, the hajji had already made it clear to Father that he wanted us to move on.

Father spoke to the group, offering his plan. "Helen and I would like

41

to try to reach the Mentawei Islands, about 600 kilometers to the north, off the Sumatra coast. I don't think the Japanese will bother to occupy these islands. The Mentawei Islanders have good, seaworthy boats capable of crossing the ocean to Australia. If we can't get a boat, we may even be able to hide on the Mentaweis for the duration of the war. Or, who knows, we may be able to get word to the Allies so they can come and pick us up. To get to the Mentaweis shouldn't be much of a problem. We ought to be able to make arrangements for a boat in one of the villages north of the Vlakke Hoek lighthouse. I want to go there anyway to find out whether there is news about the other two lifeboats . . . How many of you would like to join me in this plan?"

Not many, it appeared.

One group was determined to go to Kota Agung instead.

"But the Japs are there!" I said.

"Never mind, we're civilians. We'll be allowed to go back to friends or families on Java."

"There's a hospital in Kota Agung, so Piet can get his leg taken care of," said someone else.

"I've had enough of wandering on the sea, I don't care for any more wandering on Sumatra as Mr. Colijn has in mind."

"We'll only get sick if we go to those islands, malaria from mosquitoes, dysentery from contaminated water, and, of course, there won't be any medical care."

"You are wrong," said Father. "On the biggest island is a mission hospital."

"How do you know the missionary doctor hasn't left?

"And what if there is no boat to sail to Australia, and the Allies don't come to pick us up, we'll be stuck . . . We may have to live like Robinson Crusoe, no thank you very much."

"And what if the Japs catch us as we are trying to escape? Better to just go to Kota Agung and say 'Here we are.'"

The lifeboat arguments about what to expect of the Japanese were resumed. Several men had horror stories to tell, and I knew they were true because Father had told me some of the things the Japanese perpetrated on Tarakan—tortures, random executions, other atrocities. Every reason to try and stay out of their hands.

It was clear that the 25 people in the lifeboat would soon be going separate ways. However much we had quarreled, bickered, and argued in the boat, we had all been one. We had drunk from the same cup. We had rowed together in the sun and bailed together in the storm. We were united by the common purpose of reaching land. Now the common purpose had been served.

Fourteen men, among them Red with his dog Whiskey, and Piet, and the Javanese who had climbed the coconut tree, would sail to Kota Agung in the lifeboat, and from there go on to Java. On their way to Kota Agung, they would drop the 11 remaining people, including Father and me, at the nearest point of Sumatra's mainland. We would then walk around the Vlakke Hoek promontory to the lighthouse and decide what to do. Not all eleven were intent on going to the Mentawei Islands, but they didn't want to sail with the lifeboat right into the arms of the Japanese in Kota Agung either. What could be crazier? They would just join Mr. Colijn for a bit and see.

Definitely going with us to the Mentaweis was Mac. "I barely escaped the Japanese in Shanghai, just made it out of Java before the Japanese occupied it, and I am not going to just give myself up. I'll try to outfox them again."

Much later I learned that the only person who made it to Java was the Javanese man. The non-Asians were thrown in the Kota Agung jail and later transferred to another prison. Whiskey was bayoneted by a Japanese soldier and tossed into the sea. Piet never received treatment at a hospital. He had believed in the gentlemanly idea that in war the enemy inflicts wounds and then turns around to take care of them. This wasn't that kind of war.

Father walked over to the hajji, who had sat apart during the discussions, and told him that part of the group wanted to be dropped off at the mainland to walk to the lighthouse, and the other part would continue in the lifeboat to Kota Agung. "Could we have a guide?"

"I can show you how to get to the mainland, and then show you how to sail to Kota Agung."

"How much will it cost?"

Behind the hajji's impassive face I could guess his deliberations. Only a few weeks before, we Dutch had been the masters representing power. Now Japanese masters had taken over. If the hajji helped the beaten Dutch, the Japanese might not like it. He had given us rice, his human duty. But to assist in our escape? We would have to make it worth his while.

"I want the boat and a thousand guilders." This was the equivalent then of U.S. $400, in those days an enormous sum.

In the ways of the Far East, bargaining began. After a long, always polite discussion, the two men settled on 300 guilders plus the lifeboat, which would be turned over to the hajji upon arrival in Kota Agung. The price seemed exorbitant, but Father was eager to be on the way to find Antoinette and Alette. The 14 men who opted to sail to Kota Agung were eager to be on the way to Java.

Someone passed half a coconut shell and the 300 guilders were collected and given to Red to give to the hajji at the end of the cruise to Kota Agung.

The hajji announced he would walk back home. We could sail our boat around, drop anchor near his village, and wait for him to come aboard as our guide. But Father was not keen to let the hajji out of sight. What if he had a change of heart? Father and I would accompany him, and the three of us would then be taken to the lifeboat.

The others swam back to it, or pulled themselves across along the line. Later it was untied at the mast and left to drift toward the beach to be picked up by villagers.

On the trail to the village, silent animosity hung between Father and me and the hajji. Was he sorry he had agreed to help? Was he worried now about Japanese reprisals?

By the time we reached the village it was dark. Gruffly, he told us to sit down near a smoldering fire and wait for him. He was going home to eat.

Father gathered wood to refuel the fire, but he couldn't produce enough smoke to dispel the droves of mosquitoes.

"Wish that fellow would come and take us back to the lifeboat," I grumbled.

"We have to learn patience, Helen. We aren't in the driver's seat anymore."

The hajji returned in an even surlier mood than before; all his former politeness was gone. He led Father and me to a withered jetty and ordered us to take our places in a long, narrow outrigger sailing canoe which wobbled precariously as we stepped in. The hajji sat down in the bow. Out of the dark a slender young man in a sarong appeared and took the tiller.

The boat danced off into the black night. Spray set us nearly up to our waists in water. When I saw the lifeboat loom up, I felt a tremendous sense of security, just as I had a few days earlier after dipping into the ocean. The hajji, Father, and I climbed aboard, and the man in the sarong skittered home with the empty canoe. The breeze that made his fragile boat prance had no impact on the big clumsy sail of the lifeboat. Men had to row for two hours before we dropped anchor near a mainland beach.

One after the other the 11 of us who were not going to Kota Agung climbed overboard to wade ashore.

"Good luck in the Mentaweis, or where you're heading."

"Good luck in Kota Agung."

"Hope the Japs are nice there!"

A village was supposed to be close to the landing place, but it was pitch dark and no lights of human habitation were in sight. Still, the "wind news" seemed to have preceded us. A man emerged from the darkness and said he had been waiting for us. He was from a village some distance away. Father told him that our group would like to spend the night in that village, but the man stated firmly that he was sorry, he had no room. Like the hajji on Tabuan, he seemed eager for us to move on.

"You'll find the Belimbing lighthouse a few kilometers away. Just walk south along the coast of Semangka Bay, then around the Vlakke Hoek, and you'll arrive at the lighthouse."

"Judging from the chart in the lifeboat, that lighthouse is more than a few kilometers from here," protested the skipper to Father.

"I'm sure you are right. But we have no choice. If we can't stay in this village, we have to walk on. Maybe in the next village they'll be more hospitable."

With Father in the lead, our little group began walking along the beach. Now that the lifeboat voyage was over and he could take matters in his own hands, now that he could organize and plan, he seemed more his old vigorous self again, and I stopped worrying about *his* endurance.

How many days had it been since we had a decent night's sleep? How many days since we had a square meal? The effect of the little rice on the beach of Tabuan had long worn off. I was as hungry as I had been in the boat, but at least the thirst was gone.

High-tide water lapped right up to the undergrowth. The only place to walk was through the water, where sharp spikes of coral stabbed into my feet. It was then I realized the folly of taking off my shoes after the sinking of the *Poelau Bras*. If ever I were shipwrecked again, I would never, *never* take off my shoes. This sentiment was shared by all my barefoot companions.

No stars or moon lit our way. We had only one flashlight. We stumbled over tree roots and driftwood strewn on the beach. A few of us fell headlong into the water. We bumped our heads against overhanging tree branches. We tried to keep in touch with each other by shouting, but our hoarse cries were lost in the roar of the ocean. Every so often Father stopped to count the group. He had assumed leadership. He was the oldest. He spoke Malay the best. He was familiar with the tropical jungle. He had lived not only next to it on Tarakan but also *in* it when he worked as a geologist for the BPM on New Guinea.

It started to rain. And while I walked, the world rocked up and down. Up and down. Up and down.

Bruised, soaking wet, and faint from hunger I tottered on. What else could we do with the jungle on our right and the ocean on our left and a tide so high that the two merged in a fiendish pact? Only the thought of the lighthouse "around the corner," where there would be food, a place to wash, a bed, kept me going.

Three dismal hours went by. In a little sandy cove beyond the reach of the ocean we lay down and tried to sleep, nipped by sandflies, stung by droves of mosquitoes.

Dawn revealed a piece of nature more beautiful than any I had ever seen. The sky was a bright azure, the ocean a deep steel blue. Big towering breakers were of the purest sparkling white. The beach was also white, and sandy. And the jungle on our right was not just a forbidding, dark mass, as it had been during the night, but a rainbow of different shades of green.

"Let's go," said Father, "the lighthouse can't be far now."

Wearily, the group set out again. The skipper carried a wooden box with his sextant. In the lifeboat he had opened the box several times just to look at the instrument, the only reminder of an interrupted seafaring career. Another man clutched a brightly colored bag that had once contained California oranges and now carried letters, from his sweetheart, I assumed.

The rest of us carried nothing but wooden sticks we had picked up on the beach of Tabuan.

For several more hours we staggered on the sand, which grated our lacerated feet. As far as the eye could see stretched the sandy beach. The scene that had seemed beautiful in the morning had long lost its appeal.

"*Tuan-tuan,*" a voice called. It was the Malay word for "gentlemen," and a smiling man stepped out of the brush. Well, that's a break, I thought, someone who is glad to see us. His pleasure was derived from the discovery that we were not Japanese soldiers as he had thought. Even though we were Dutch, he extended his hospitality in his village, a few thatched huts on stilts scattered among trees not far from the beach. Twenty-five men lived here. Our local spokesman didn't include women in the count.

At the friendly man's invitation, we all went up the ladder of his hut and entered a room containing two bamboo platforms, or *balai-balai's*, about 50 centimeters off the ground, beds of the parents and the children.

A shy woman came from the back and spread an eating mat on the floor. She placed bowls of rice and salted fish on it for each of us and her husband. Before she left again, she served tea in white bowls that had a fancy floral pattern and were stamped "made in Japan."

As I ate I recalled the days in 1939 when Antoinette and I had just arrived in the East Indies and visited marketplaces on Java. How unappetizing we new arrivals had thought the native foods looked. And how absolutely wonderful this rice and salted fish tasted now, after our awful trek.

Children peered through holes in the *gedék*—the bamboo-plaited wall. The man told Father that only white male Dutch civil servants had come to the village, and then only occasionally. This was the first time the children had seen a white woman.

After the meal, our host left and returned with a pile of faded, worn sarongs. "You can borrow these to bathe in." He preceded us down the ladder, a short distance through the bushes, to the bank of a little murky river. Here we left our clothes after donning the sarongs. This took some doing in our Dutch/American group. Father was used to bathing in rivers this way, but some of the sailors of the *Poelau Bras* had never had occasion to be near a sarong, let alone drape one on.

They were men's sarongs, sewn together at the sides to make a wide tube to step into, fold double over the waist, and then tightly roll down over the top so the sarong fitted snugly around the waist. I was so busy doing just that, except I was making my roll under my armpits, that I only saw out of the corner of my eye that several men were modestly dropping their shorts or pants *after* the sarong was in place. In doing so they loosened the sarong roll and had to start the process all over again. Mac was one of the strugglers. Later he laughed about it and said, "A sarong made Dorothy Lamour, but it only covers me—once I know how to keep the thing in place, that is."

The brown water of the river flowed slowly by the bank. I waded in waist-deep. Mud oozed between my toes. At first I held onto the top of the sarong with one hand, afraid the roll might come undone and leave me standing there in my bra. But the lukewarm water was so comforting and soothing that I released my hold on the sarong and followed the example of others. I squatted down, keeping just my head above water, popped up again, splashed water over me with my hands, squatted down again, scrubbed myself. I stopped enjoying myself when I saw feces floating by. I returned to the river bank. Still dressed in the sarong, I rinsed the salt and sand out of my khaki outfit and put it on again.

In serious silence or with nervous little giggles, a group of small children who had watched us bathe now stared after us as we marched back, single file, to the village. The very little children were naked and wore lobster claws on pieces of string around their necks to ward off evil spirits. Older ones wore only grubby cotton shirts which tipped up in front over round little bellies.

Upon leaving the village after a few hours' sleep on the floor of the hut where we had our meal, we now also carried one battered enamel kettle for boiling water, an enamel cup, four gourds with carrying loops of jungle vine that held water already boiled, several banana leaf packages of cooked rice, and a save-until-we-are-really-hungry-again bunch of bananas.

When our friend in the village assured us that the lighthouse was just a little farther along the coast, we all had our doubts about his accuracy. But we were heartened to learn that in the jungle near the lighthouse nine white oil men had built a refuge. Father thought they might be BPM men. "Maybe *they* have news about Antoinette and Alette."

With him in the lead once more, the 11 of us started walking along the beach. It was now four o'clock in the afternoon of March 14.

Suddenly it was dark, the way it gets dark in the tropics, without warning, without transition from day to night. We stopped for dinner. Men arranged sticks as a tripod, filled the kettle with water from a stream, gathered wood, made a fire, and hung the kettle from the tripod. I unwrapped the banana leaf packages, and we all dipped our fingers into the rice, rolled it into balls and popped them into our mouths. When the water boiled, Mac made tea with the leaves he had been carrying in a piece of old newspaper, together with matches, and we each drank in turn from the enamel cup

We walked the whole night. Always, rounding a bend in the coastline, I was sure I would see the lighthouse. Always, there was only an empty stretch of wide, sandy beach, tinted an eerie greyish white in the clear tropical night. Always, I had the feeling of not belonging, of floating between the jungle, stretching for kilometers and kilometers over Sumatra, and the Indian Ocean, stretching for kilometers and kilometers to Antarctica.

I thought of our family walks along the beaches of Holland. Father would say to us children in a nice, cheery way, "Now we want to reach Katwijk (or Noordwijk or some other place on the North Sea), and we are not going to sit down to rest every few minutes. We are going to walk without stopping for 50 minutes, and then rest for 10 minutes, and walk again for 50 minutes. That's the way they do it in the military."

Father was mobilized for the first time in World War I when The Netherlands was able to maintain neutrality but kept young men like Father under arms. So in the 1930s, we three girls would brace ourselves against the wind (we always seemed to walk against the wind) and plod along "in military fashion" toward our goal, where waffles with cream in a café might be offered as a reward for a walk well done.

Now Father was setting the pace on a Sumatra beach and I noticed that he treated his grown-up daughter and the men who had quite recently been officers or personnel in the merchant marine or Royal Netherlands East Indies Forces, and a war correspondent for United Press, in nearly the same way he had treated his three little girls on the Dutch beach.

Hour after hour we trudged on over the moonlit sand—blocks of 50 long minutes of walking with 10 minutes rest in between, when sandflies nipped and mosquitoes stung. My feet throbbed harder, muscles ached more whenever I staggered up from a rest, and invariably Father would say, "I'm sure *this* march will bring the lighthouse."

His good humor was shared by few of the others. I wonder now why all these men, many of them strong and independent, decided to follow him. They surely could have traveled on their own. But they, too, must have felt themselves to be floating between the jungle and the ocean with nowhere to go. It was impossible to go back. Ahead was only escape or capture. There was safety in numbers.

Father was everyone's senior by years. He was nearing 50. What gave him the strength to go on? A partial answer must have been his lifelong physical training—swims in cold seas, climbs of arduous mountains. But perhaps more sustaining were his strong, deep faith in God and his unshakable conviction that he would find Antoinette and Alette—in the direction we were walking.

We walked, rested, ate the last food, including the precious bananas, walked, rested, walked until the new day broke. The lighthouse was still not in sight. After one rest pause Father said to me as I was scrambling up, "You keep resting. I'm sure the others will be only too happy to keep you company. I'll go ahead and see whether this famous lighthouse is anywhere near now."

I lay down again. Vaguely, I registered that Mac went along with Father. From the others came not a word. They were already asleep.

It couldn't have been long before I heard someone say, "Mac is coming back."

"Cheer up," he said, "this time the lighthouse *is* just around the corner."

We all got up, rounded one more bend in the Sumatra coastline, and there it was, a graceful, slender tower glistening white against the blue sky. From behind a heavy fort-like wall rose a thin column of smoke. Father was almost there already, and as we watched, he disappeared behind the wall. Reaching the lighthouse, which was to have been a few hours' walk from where the lifeboat dropped us off, had taken 20 hours of toil.

I stood still and gazed at the lighthouse and the smoke column. What could they be cooking? Father came out again and jogged toward us. I could tell he had good news. Was it possible he had news of Antoinette and Alette?

I moved on and soon outdistanced the others. Half an hour before, I had been sure I couldn't take another step. Now I was fairly running.

Father shouted something, but his voice was lost in the pounding of the surf. He swung his arms over his head and clasped his hands together. He walked faster. I walked faster, too. When there were only a few yards between us he said simply, "Antoinette and Alette are safe."

"Oh," I said. And the two of us stood there on the lonely beach and said no more. Too much had happened in too little time for us to take it all in in a normal way. Just as I had watched the people jumping overboard without worrying about them, I now stood on the beach and, upon hearing that my two lost sisters had survived the shipwreck, I said "Oh. Where are they?"

"Until a few hours ago they were at the lighthouse with the others from their lifeboat, 33 people in all. Their boat landed toward the north, and they all came down here, but then they left in a hurry, went north again when they heard that a Japanese patrol was marching up from the south."

"A Japanese patrol . . .?"

"Yes," and a twinkle I hadn't seen in Father's eyes for a long, long time was back. "Us. Apparently, natives spotted our group and mistook us for the Japanese Army, just like the man in that friendly village did. The survivors from the second lifeboat are hiding in the jungle with the oil people we heard about. They are indeed from the BPM. The girls, according to the lighthouse warden, seemed to be all right, except that Antoinette had her arm in a sling. One man of their boat, a crew member of the *Poelau Bras*, stayed behind in the lighthouse when the others left. He died."

"Let's go and surprise the girls right away," I suggested.

"We'll have to wait until tomorrow. We'll need a guide to show us the trail to the jungle camp, and today none is available. The delay will give us time to take a bath and rest."

Another bath—it sounded delicious. Once more I wrapped a borrowed sarong around me and this time, with soap in hand, stood near a well drawing bucket after bucket of clear water to wash away the latest sand and salt. I also washed Father's and my "Java clothes" and spread them out on the cobblestones to dry.

Under a faded moth-eaten Dutch flag in the lighthouse lay the dead crew member of the *Poelau Bras*. In the evening we buried him. The warden had made a coffin. Four men from my boat carried it to a grave dug under a palm tree. After Father said a short prayer, the warden and Dutch people from my boat sang a Dutch hymn and Mac sang "Abide with me."

And then I slept in the sarong in a four-poster bed with a mosquito net draped over it.

Our guide the next day couldn't have been more than ten years old, but he carried a large *parang* in one hand. For three hours Father and I followed him along the beach. Then he stopped short before a pond. Pointing to the jungle that still lined the beach, as it had since we left the lifeboat, he said, "That's where we're going." He started splashing through the pond and pointed to a barely visible narrow trail entering the jungle. Here, finally, he could proudly swing his parang and cut branches and lianas to clear the path.

Sunlight filtered through only sparsely. Often the trail was like a tunnel through a mysterious world where unseen birds called, twittered, and sang, crickets chirped, and other, unimaginable creatures made noises. Suddenly, in such a tunnel, we came upon two barefoot girls dressed in black.

And that's how Father and I met up with Antoinette and Alette, on a trail deep in a Sumatra jungle. They were walking there because someone in the camp announced that two white persons were approaching, and the girls thought these people might have news about Father and me.

"It was like a miracle," Antoinette reminisced recently, "an apparition. Here you and Father came strolling down the jungle trail behind a small boy swinging an enormous parang. You were alive!"

It was a scene right out of a movie, but we didn't act as the movie would probably have portrayed us, with exclamations of joy and relief, with tears and embraces. We were still watching the drama of our lives instead of living it.

We talked casually, as if we had just met at a bus stop.

"But what are you girls wearing?" I asked. They wore cotton calf-length pants that, at a later time in fashion, would be called pedal-pushers, and cotton jackets that tied in front. "You look like our gardener on Java."

"Our clothes were such a mess," said Antoinette. "We left them at the lighthouse. The warden gave us these clothes, they were worn by coolies of his."

"Did you have a shave at the lighthouse, Father? You look so spruced up," said Alette. "Most of the men from our boat are still walking around with their ten-day-old beards."

"You should see the houses the BPM people built in the camp," said Antoinette, "marvelous stilted things made from bamboo and palm leaves and tied together with lianas. Not one nail in the whole camp. I feel sorry for them, though. They had enough supplies to last for a year, and probably could have stayed hidden from the Japanese. But with all of us shipwreck survivors piling in on them, the food won't last long, and, anyway, such masses are bound to be discovered. Think of it. There were only nine of them, but then 33 people from our boat descended on them. Oh no, 32, one of them died. And now you two, and nine more to come from the lighthouse."

"We'd better move along," said Father, and motioned to our guide, who was patiently sitting on his haunches on the trail. "You two go first, you already know the way." Before they started he gave each of them a tender pat on the shoulder.

Soon we reached the camp in a clearing where the sun was shining and men were laughing as they bathed in the clear stream.

And it was while sitting on a boulder in this stream that the four of us talked about our lifeboat voyages. But we were merely trading details then, little odds and ends that seemed amusing to tell. The stark horror of my sisters' lifeboat voyage I only pieced together over many years, for it was always difficult for them to talk about.

After we four jumped off the *Poelau Bras* into our assigned lifeboat and the exploding bomb nearby cascaded water over us, Antoinette's leg, she thinks, became jammed between one of the water tanks and the side of the boat. She noticed it when Father called, "Antoinette, Alette, get out of the boat, swim away as fast as you can." In vain, Alette tried to free Antoinette's leg.

The lifeboat was still close to the burning ship, a ship that would soon be sinking, and Antoinette and Alette desperately wanted to leave the small craft.

"You go alone, Alette," said Antoinette.

"Don't be silly. Of course we'll stay together."

A Japanese machine-gunner aimed at the lifeboat occupants. Shrapnel tore Antoinette's left arm open from the elbow to the wrist. Alette was hit in the back. The ensuing pain blurred the girls' memories.

Alette remembers seeing that a blond woman next to her was also hit, "a hideous shoulder wound. She kept on looking at it and saying, 'How will it ever be repaired?' She must have been in awful pain, but she never winced or let out so much as a whimper."

Antoinette remembers the tat-tat-tat-tat-tat of another volley just as she was saying something to comfort the injured woman and thinks she herself must have received shrapnel in the neck, because she had wounds under her jaw and her vocal chords were paralyzed, but her teeth were not damaged. Later she said, "If I hadn't been talking, if my mouth had been closed, the shrapnel might have killed me." Yet another volley killed the woman next to Alette.

Antoinette lost consciousness and when she awoke, the *Poelau Bras* was gone. Of Father and me there was no sign. After the boat had filled up again with survivors, the blond woman was put overboard.

A man looked at Antoinette and said, "She's gone too. Let's get rid of her."

Antoinette wanted to scream, "I'm not dead," but she could not speak.

A man bent over her, felt her pulse, looked at the blood-splashed face and at the eyes that were unable to send a signal, and said, "She is dead, no use keeping an extra body in the boat."

Alette doesn't recall hearing this, although she was sitting close to Antoinette, and thinks she too must have lost consciousness for a while. They never knew who saved Antoinette from being tossed into the sea.

Of the first few days of the lifeboat voyage my sisters remember mostly their pain, and Antoinette also her inability to speak. There were other small but important memories. Antoinette recalls that when the water went around, someone patiently used her ration to wet her lips and tongue, dabbing the water on with a handkerchief, for she was unable to swallow. A sailor with a front tooth missing and a squint combed her hair. Someone else rubbed her bare feet during the cold nights. Neither of the girls had shoes, but they can't recall how and when they took them off. Next to Antoinette, with his feet to her face, lay a man who couldn't control his bladder because he had been shot through the belly. Several times the voice belonging to the feet apologized for the acrid, penetrating stench. Antoinette says he might have been the crew member Father and I helped bury under the palm tree at the lighthouse.

Alette remembers most vividly that at the beginning of the voyage someone told her that I had been killed and put overboard. But when Alette six days later was given a set of rings, "These belonged to your sister," they included a wedding ring. Then she knew the rings must have belonged to the blond woman who sat next to her during the machine-gunning, and Helen might still be alive.

This revelation came shortly before landing. By then Alette's shrapnel wounds had almost healed. Antoinette was lucid and regaining her ability to speak. Since they told few details in the jungle bivouac, it wasn't until years later that I found out how serious their injuries were and marveled at their rapid recovery.

Antoinette did go into some detail about her arm when Father asked about it. "No one knew whether it was broken, so, just to be on the safe side, someone splinted it with a piece of wood chiseled out of the lifeboat. It was a heavy piece. That's why Alette supported my arm most of the walk to this jungle camp. Each day in the lifeboat someone put salt water compresses on the arm. They kept away infection, and the sea air was clean. Now that we are on land, infection has set in."

As she said it, I became aware of a sickening putrid smell. She saw me wrinkle my nose, and said, "That's my arm."

"We have to get that arm healed," worried Father. "I'm going to pay someone to go to the villages further north and find sulfa. That ought to stop the infection. The wound will probably leave a scar. When the war is over, I'll buy you a beautiful bracelet to cover it."

"Talking about injuries," Father continued matter-of-factly, "what about doing something about those little leech-wounds we have all collected. Helen's legs are the worst."

I looked at my blood-streaked legs. The trail to the camp had been full of leeches. In the past, those nasty, sleazy little worms had been the bane of my jungle expeditions, but then I had been properly dressed—with hiking boots, the very ones I had so imprudently pulled off in the Indian Ocean, and socks to my knees. Leeches that did find a spot of skin to settle on, I got rid of quickly with a burning cigarette from a pack I carried for that purpose. This time, of course, I was barefoot, had bare legs, and no cigarettes. And I didn't have the discipline to let the leeches sit on my skin and become so fat that they fell off on their own, as I knew I was supposed to do. Instead, every time I became aware that another leech had fastened onto me, I gripped the worm between thumb and index, always feeling a little shudder, and pulled it off to toss into the jungle. Then the leech was gone, and another little bleeding leg wound had taken its place.

For a while we all sat with our legs in the running water of the stream, hoping to soak the wounds clean. "Let's hope they don't get infected," said Antoinette. "No one has medicine to spare around here."

Back on our boulder, we watched the other shipwreck survivors splashing in the river, preparing food, or simply lying on their own rocks or on the riverbank and enjoying being alive.

"We'd better start talking about the future," said Father. "I want to know what you three think."

He unfolded his Mentawei plans to Antoinette and Alette, and we talked for a long time about the wisdom of going there. On the one hand, the mission hospital was probably still operating, and there probably would be a doctor. But if there were complications to Antoinette's arm or Alette's back, specialized treatment and medication might not be available even there. And we might have to live for months on inadequate foods, exposing our weakened bodies to malaria and dysentery. On the other hand, the alternative was most certainly capture.

"We must do everything we can so you won't be caught," said Antoinette. "I'm for the plan."

"Me too," said Alette. "If we can get to those islands and then to Australia, we can at least do something to help the war effort."

"This way we can stay together," I said. "If we get captured, we may be separated." I thought about Mother already a captive on Tarakan.

"So you think we should try, you think trying to stay out of Japanese hands is worth the potential hardships and risks to our health?"

"Yes, indeed," said Alette.

"Of course," said Antoinette.

"You bet," said I.

Chapter Five

Capture

"I'm afraid that man pedaling toward us looks Japanese," I said, dropping my remark into an already long silence on the porch of the Ngambur rest house.

The others followed my gaze—Father, my two sisters, Mac, and Mr. Oosten, a BPM colleague of Father's. He was in my sisters' lifeboat and had joined in the Mentawei Islands escape plan.

The man bicycling down the village road wore a khaki shirt and breeches and tall riding boots. He must be an officer, I thought to myself, noting a long, slightly curved leather sheath hanging at his side. I pictured the sharp samurai sword I had read about.

Three other men on bicycles followed. They wore baggy shorts down to their knees and sloppy puttees over worn combat boots. These must be common soldiers. They had visored caps with flaps in back to protect their necks from the tropical sun. No one on the porch said a word. Our escape attempts had failed. We were about to be captured.

We had not expected the Japanese here in Ngambur, although we knew they had established a military post in Krui, the small port less than

50 kilometers to the north. Two weeks ago, in the jungle bivouac close to the Belimbing lighthouse, a comfortable 140 kilometers had separated us from Krui. But in order to find the hoped-for sailing boat for our escape, we had had to travel to villages farther north, ever closer to Krui. In dark corners of villages Father had argued passionately with native boat owners. "Not here, maybe the next village," all had said, and we had been forced to travel on.

Along the beach and up and down muddy jungle trails we walked or were shaken about in rickety little rented two-wheeled carts, each pulled by a puny one-humped ox. The carts held barely two passengers amid the drivers' pots and pans and other personal belongings under a palm-frond canopy.

"Every time we leave the beach, the highest demands are made upon our shock-absorbing capability," I observed weeks later in the diary I kept of the shipwreck and journey to the camp. "I'm amazed at the apparent ease with which the oxen pull their loads through the mud and up the hills—and at the endurance of the oxcarts themselves. The wheels sometimes are scarily slanted, but they never collapse. We do have to get out of the carts regularly to slosh through the mud, and we have to stop traveling when the sun sets. The drivers say we can't travel in the dark because of elephants."

We slept on the beach, pelted by nipping sandflies, or on mats on the floor in village homes, surrounded by buzzing mosquitoes. Once my sisters and I shared a big bed with a lumpy mattress in a guest house that, to our Dutch eyes, seemed incredibly dirty, probably from lack of use.

On our trek to Ngambur, we had crossed several muddy rivers that flow from the Bukit Barisan mountains and empty into the Indian Ocean. First, the oxen were unharnessed so they could swim across. Then the carts, their wheels in the water, were set on a dug-out canoe poled across by the oxcart driver or pulled along a ferry rope. Finally, we went across in the dug-out canoe. By that time the oxen on the other side had wandered off into the undergrowth.

We had rejoiced in abundant rice and the diversity of fruit available when we reached more prosperous areas, but the rejoicing made me feel guilty. "It's an awful feeling to attach so much value to material things, but I can't seem to rise above it," I wrote. "I dream every night and half the day of good meals and well-prepared dishes. The first papaya in Ngaras, the first sweet potato with butter and fried eggs in Ngambur, gave color to an entire day. And then I have visions of a bed, just for me, of snow-white sheets, of a bathroom with a clean towel, instead of those dirty rivers where I bathe wrapped in a sarong while the entire village gawks."

With every day that we failed to find a boat to sail to the Mentaweis, we knew our chances of being captured were multiplying. Not only were we getting physically closer to Krui, where the Japanese were, but we were hearing tales of other small groups of shipwreck survivors traveling the same coastal route. Surely the Japanese in Krui were aware of the sudden influx of *Poelau Bras* survivors, all of them knocking at the doors of local inhabitants for food or a place to sleep and shopping at the little village stores for soap, a toothbrush or something to wear.

One story came to us of the landing of a third lifeboat with 54 survivors. This was tremendously good news, but the group was met by a party of Japanese and had had to surrender en masse. They were now being sent to a prison camp somewhere. Rumor had it that all the whites in the area—men, women, and children—were being rounded up.

We six in Ngambur knew all this, but still we had counted on getting a boat that evening. The headman in the village had promised Father one. We were to be called to sail at midnight.

"Think of it," Antoinette had mused earlier, "by this time tomorrow we may be out on the open sea again."

"What if the headman backs out? He may have second thoughts. He may be too afraid to help us after all," said Alette.

"But Father is offering him a handsome sum," I threw in.

"Won't do him much good if the Japanese chop his head off."

And now four Japanese characters in their odd-fitting uniforms were coming up the steps of the porch.

The officer unbuckled his sheathed sword and put it in a corner. The boy who had been filling our orders at the guest house came running with a rattan chair for him.

"Have no chairs, no chairs!" the boy had told us, and we'd all been sitting in a row, tailor-fashion, with legs stretched straight ahead, on the planked porch, our backs leaning against the room's *gedék*, plaited bamboo wall. The boy now wore a batiked head cloth. He had covered his head as

59

a sign of respect for the Japanese, just as local men had done for us a short while ago, according to their *adat*, their customs law. It was these mundane details that suddenly brought home the fact that our snug colonial world was coming to an end. There were new rulers in the Netherlands East Indies.

The soldiers slung their rifles off their backs and propped the weapons in front of them, muzzles pointing upward. To my relief they had no bayonets on their rifles.

Only then did the officer speak. "Good morning," he said, in English. Clearly and politely, Father returned the greeting, but the rest of us made only barely audible sounds.

Mr. Oosten hid his head behind a two-year-old American newspaper he had bought in one of the little village shops. Such papers were shipped from the U.S. and sent to remote villages like Ngambur to be used as wrapping paper or to cover the gedék walls of the native huts. I could tell Mr. Oosten was not reading, but listening to the conversation.

Mac made the pretense of writing in an exercise book, which he had already half filled with copious notes. "The beginning of a series of news-paper articles, or maybe a book, as soon as we get onto and off those Mentawei Islands," he had said. Of course, he, too, was listening. He was lucky the conversation was in English.

Alette started to wind a newly purchased bandage around Antoinette's extended arm. She had just treated Antoinette's shrapnel wound with an-other salt water compress, for we had found no sulfa to treat it. Both girls kept their faces blank. They don't want to show the Japanese how they feel, I thought. We had all been raised to keep our feelings to ourselves. I had nothing in my hands to occupy me, so I deliberately gazed past the Japa-nese at the local men who had gathered below the porch to see how the former masters were being treated. They stood in silence. These men, too, were wearing their batiked head cloths or *pici's*, the rimless black velvet caps of the Muslims.

The officer's English was poor. Laboriously he wrote down everything Father said.

"Your name?"

"Anton Hendrik Colijn."

"Age?"

"Forty-seven."

"These girls?"

"My daughters."

"Names."

"Helena Constantia, Antoinette, Alette Cornelia."

"Ages."

"Twenty-one, twenty, sixteen."

The man started gathering similar information from the others, then suddenly pointed to Antoinette and asked, "Why bandage girl's arm?"

"A Japanese pilot shot at her when she was in a lifeboat."

"I am sorry," said this Japanese officer, and he gave an order to one of the soldiers, who returned to his bicycle and came back with a medicine kit. He unwound the bandage that Alette had just wrapped around Antoinette's arm and cleaned the raw, pus-dripping wound with cotton and tweezers. Then he sprinkled the wound with white powder that must have been the long-sought-after sulfa powder. Finally, he wound her arm with a new bandage of his own. Through it all, Antoinette stared stoically ahead.

The interrogation continued. The officer focused on Father again.

"Where did you work?"

"Borneo," said Father. Good, I thought, an enormous island. I hope he doesn't ask where on Borneo. Tarakan will remind the man of oil, of the Japanese taking the island. He may have heard of hostages who had escaped.

"Your profession?"

"Geologist." Good going, I cheered silently. Father hadn't worked in the field for years, but a geologist was not so high up as "manager."

I was getting anxious, though. The officer was bound to realize soon that Father was a military man. If he didn't deduce this from the interrogation, he had only to look at Father's clothes. True, the shirt was stripped of insignia, and there were no Netherlands Lions on his field uniform buttons, but the shorts and shirt still had the cut and the green color of a uniform of the Royal Netherlands East Indies Army.

Mr. Oosten must have sensed how anxious I was, and how afraid to betray my anxiety, for he handed me a piece of his newspaper. The print of *The New York Times* blurred before my eyes as I listened hard to the droning dialogue and stole glances at the four enemy men.

The face of the officer was inscrutable, as Westerners said the Japanese to be. He did have some polish and displayed some humanity—a sharp contrast to the soldiers. These men fit nowhere in the image I had of a Japan of exquisite porcelains, carefully raked gardens, delicate flower arrangements, and tea ceremonies. It was possible to picture the officer wearing a kimono and bowing before a statue in his home. I could only picture the others putting bayonets on their rifles to butcher prisoners and then laughing about it, as they had done on Tarakan.

I looked cautiously at Antoinette and saw the corners of her mouth turn up. Oh, no, I thought. I hope she isn't going to have a giggling fit. When we were small, we had often giggled together until we were in tears of laughter and I wet my pants. Now I caught from her the urge to start giggling, too. But there was nothing to laugh at, I thought, nothing at all. Here we all sat uncomfortably on the floor, and in the comfort of a rattan chair sat a man who held our fate in his hands, flanked by three creatures whom I felt sure wouldn't hesitate to kill us if so ordered.

I composed myself, and Antoinette did too. She must have realized that she was not going to determine our fate with a fit of nervous laughter.

Finally, the officer said to Father, "You all report to Krui tomorrow."

"We can't get there so soon. Most of us can hardly walk," Father protested, and he waved a hand at the bandaged feet on the porch—infection of the coral and bloodsucker wounds had set in. "We have to travel in oxcarts, and they are very slow."

The officer wrote something in Japanese on a piece of paper and gave Father what presumably was a deferment pass.

"Two days," he said.

The photo the officer took of us before leaving the next day is one I would very much have liked to seen (and I've wondered since if it isn't filed away somewhere in an archive in Japan). He had us all six stand in a row, and we all stood as straight as we could, assuming looks of scorn and pride. Antoinette and Alette wore their black "gardener" pants. I had on my "Java clothes"—the khaki shirt and shorts I was shipwrecked in. Father and Mr. Oosten wore new shirts and sarongs, purchased after the officer had left the previous day. Mac was a character right out of a Gilbert and Sullivan operetta—a straight reed wrapped in a maroon-plaid sarong. He also wore a white pith helmet and a white jacket with a standup collar too small to button. He carried his old clothes and newly bought possessions in a wicker basket.

In these outfits we headed for Krui, traveling in two oxcarts. Each cart held two passengers, so the six of us took turns sitting. As the only one without festering foot wounds or diarrhea, I walked all the way. At one point, walking ahead of the oxcarts, I came upon a scene that struck me as only mildly surprising at the time. In light of subsequent events, I have come to consider it a small miracle. It was at one of the river crossings: a local woman had spread a plaited mat on the grass and set out six empty enamel bowls, serving bowls filled with rice and vegetables, and a platter of fried bananas. A Japanese officer had come by her house, she told me, and ordered her to have a meal ready for our party of six.

We spent the night in the house of a local man in Tandjung Stia who before the occupation had held a Dutch government post. The next morning I rented a bicycle and pedaled away over a good dirt road to arrange for our new lodgings.

Sometimes, when I ride my bike now, so many years later, I think about that 20-kilometer barefoot ride to Krui past palm trees, rice fields, flowering hibiscus, women washing clothes in a stream, and children playing naked nearby. How wonderful it was, even though I was sweaty and covered with dust, and even though in one village people jeered. At that place I didn't dare ask to buy a coconut to quench my thirst.

In another village I was invited into a home and offered rice and salted fish and hot *sambal*, chili pepper paste. The village head came in and asked how His Excellency Colijn was, and this disturbed me. Apparently the *kabar angin*, the wind news, had preceded us again. "The son of the former Dutch prime minister had been on the *Poelau Bras*, and now was on his way to Krui." It would be hard to keep Father's military past from the Japanese if all the locals here knew who he was. Some Japanese military man would put two and two together and latch on to Father's role on Tarakan.

I poured out these fears in my diary, but I also wrote this: "It was a radiant day when I traveled with my pocket full of peanuts, and toiletries tied in a sarong. I felt wonderfully light, a free bird on a bicycle, and full of joy."

Close to Krui, locals warned me that the Japanese were in town. However, I saw none about before I arrived at the home of the Herrebrugh family. Mr. Herrebrugh was a Dutch agent for the Koninklijke Pakketvaart Maatschappij, the shipping line that maintained service between the islands of the Dutch East Indies.

I leaned the bicycle against a wall, removed the sarong bundle from the handle bars, and padded in just in time to be invited to join the couple for dinner. Three small children were tended by a local woman in another room.

"A nicely laid table with white table cloth and complete covers," I reported in my diary. "To this were added the pleasures of a lighthouse nearby, the perfect setting for observing the magnificent sunset, and a bathroom."

I was just enjoying the privacy, the clean water, the soap, when there was a knock at the door and Mrs. Herrebrugh told me that a note had arrived for her husband. "Please come to my office with Miss Helena at once. Japanese officer."

So it is starting, I thought. I am being ordered around. I'll have to do as I'm told. I went with Mr. Herrebrugh, and was ushered into the presence of the same officer who had intruded upon us two days before.

He was now sitting behind a desk. Again, he was friendly, but this time he had a soldier with him who translated his Japanese into Malay. My Malay wasn't that fluent, but when he formally asked how we all were, I managed to convey, via the interpreter, that my sister was running a fever because of infection in her arm. The officer again said he was sorry. He was eager to see the other oil man because he was an engineer (and how did he know that? I wondered; this hadn't come up during the interrogation in Ngambur two days ago), and the Japanese army needed engineers. Probably to repair all those oil installations that had been destroyed, I thought. As far as Father and we girls were concerned, the officer continued, he saw no reason why we couldn't return to Java. Of course, we should recuperate first. Maybe we could go to Liwa in the mountains. (My father had proposed this in Ngambur.)

I left the officer at his desk, and walked alone back to my hosts' house. Imagine a Japanese being this nice, I marveled. He didn't even send a soldier to escort me. Liwa sounded good. Maybe we would be left in peace after all.

Earlier I had sought out a Chinese tailor and ordered a grey-sleeved shirt and shorts of the same cotton material. These were delivered to me at the Herrebrughs' house a few hours later. I had already borrowed clothes from my hosts and sent mine to a Chinese laundryman. He returned them beautifully washed and ironed at my next address, a Dutch government rest house where I made arrangements for our party to stay. Briefly the old world was back—a tailor, a laundryman, and a respectable inn to spend the night.

The others were tired when they arrived from traveling all day in the oxcarts. But they had stopped at a Japanese clinic, where Antoinette's arm had been treated again and the bandages of the others had been changed.

In a lovely reminder of a world already far away, I slept in a bed with white sheets and a mosquito net, a bed I shared with Antoinette. Father and Alette were in another bed nearby. My feeling of joy was shattered when I heard the clock at a nearby tower strike one. One a.m.! According to my watch, it was only eleven-thirty. Krui was already on their *Nippon* time. As if in protest, the watch stopped soon after.

The next morning, two cars full of Japanese officers stopped with a loud honking of horns in front of the inn. Following them was a stake truck full of soldiers. Some 30 of them spilled out and swarmed over the rooms, examining furniture, poking bayonets in wall pictures, and staring at us. Eight officers positioned themselves in a semi-circle around my father, my sisters, and me. Fortunately, we were already dressed. They began another interrogation. These men spoke only a little Malay, and there was no interpreter.

"You, tomorrow, Benkulen," one of them said to Father.

Benkulen was a coastal city much farther north. We had no desire to go there. We wanted to go south to Java.

"No," Father said, and he spoke Malay slowly, emphasizing every word. "No, other officer say to my daughter we go to Liwa, not Benkulen. Liwa, then Java," and he pointed in the direction of Java, and to all the bandages. He put his hand on Antoinette's forehead to indicate she had a fever.

But Benkulen it was to be—there was no misunderstanding that. We were told to take what we wanted from the rest house. This was an immense favor granted to only a very few, we later discovered. Father told us, "Take the mosquito nets. Hang onto them whatever happens."

"What about you?" said Antoinette.

"I'll be all right, you take them. These two are large enough to cut into three."

So my sisters and I pulled the nets off the two large beds and were about to start on the sheets when the soldiers came milling into the room again and, with grunts and completely unintelligible sounds but with imperative waves of the hand, made it clear that my sisters, Father, and I were to go outside.

In front of the inn we found Mac and Mr. Oosten, who had shared a room. A little farther up the street stood the Herrebrugh family amid their luggage. It seemed to be true, all the whites were rounded up. I waved to them, and didn't see them again for more than two years.

Our little shipwreck party didn't go north to Benkulen, after all. We went to Liwa in the mountains, but not to recuperate, as the kind officer had suggested. We were taken to Liwa in a rattling Japanese-chauffeured bus with four Dutch families from the Krui area: four mothers, eight children, and two fathers. The other two men had been called for military duty and, if not dead, were now prisoners of war somewhere, but the wives had no news. The children were all preschool or grade-school age. Families living in the outer districts of the Dutch East Indies often sent children of high-school age for their schooling to Java, as Alette had been, or left them in Holland to board with a family, as happened to Antoinette and me.

One of the mothers obviously had had time to prepare for departure from her home. She had dragged two mattresses onto the bus and a number of valises that I imagined were sensibly filled. Another mother was less lucky. "They didn't even want to give me a chance to go back to the kitchen and throw some canned goods in a hamper." Her little daughter, a blond five-year-old with big blue eyes, whimpered, "I want my teddy bear." Her mother tried to comfort her. "I left him at home to watch our house for us. You'll find him waiting for you when we return." She explained to me softly, "I knew she would ask for the bear. It's all beaten up, but she always takes him to bed with her, an animal to cuddle. I was so rattled when those brutes came for us, I packed her fancy doll with a porcelain head and lace gown. Well, she can't cuddle Eugenie."

Alette asked the little girl, "Do you want me to play a game with you?" The two played a finger game, the Dutch equivalent of "This is the church, this is the steeple."

Liwa is only 35 kilometers from Krui, but with many stops and starts it took the Japanese bus all afternoon. At every little settlement local children waved paper flags with red suns on them and cheered, "Nippon, Nippon." From houses flew flags with the rising sun.

"I hate to see all those Japanese flags," I said.

"Don't look at them then," said Antoinette crossly.

It was the only thing she said during our first day of transport. Normally, she was the most talkative of us three. *Ritje-me-fitje* we called her in the family, a term not found in the standard Dutch dictionary. To us it meant someone who acts, and talks, fast. Today she was obviously too much in pain to chatter.

At various times during the ride stops, the men in our group, thinking they would carry more authority than we women—who, as we all knew, didn't count for as much as the men with the Japanese— asked what exactly their plans were for us. They always said they didn't know. And maybe they didn't. The Japanese Army had occupied a huge area with some 100,000 non-Asian civilians who were to be put in camps. Had someone in Tokyo made a master plan?

"A firm plan cannot be detected," I wrote, "If one Japanese gives an order, you can be absolutely sure the next one will give a counter-order." I had little reason to change this observation during the three-and-a-half years I was to spend in the hands of the occupying Japanese Army.

On this evening of April 3, 1942, the Japanese billeted all of us in the house of a Dutchman who had held an administrative post in the colonial government and had been excused from military service. "All government officials are to stay at their posts," the Governor-General had ordered when the Netherlands East Indies entered the war with Japan. Just before we arrived, the Japanese had told this official he too would have to leave his house. He decided to make the most of his available food supplies and had his cook prepare a banquet for the crowd. I was still sufficiently preoccupied with prewar niceties that I wrote in my diary, "He ran out of wine, so we had to drink vermouth with dinner."

That night we all spread out on the floor and the furniture (an easy chair made a great child's bed). Before the sun rose the next morning, the Japanese came stomping through the house telling us we all had to get ready to go to Palembang, a town all the way across Sumatra on the southeast coast. We would have to assemble there "for interrogation." Other captured men, women, and children joined us.

The Japanese now began a process they would repeat twice more before we reached our final destination in Palembang: separating the men
from the women and children. This was a haphazard and lengthy proce-
dure, involving orders and counter-orders. Finally, all the men were in one
open truck and the women in another. Since all of us assumed we would
surely be reunited at the end of the day, there were no teary farewells.

En route Father waved to the three of us as we sprawled with other
women and their children on the bed of our truck, "draped around a Japanese soldier on a rattan chair," I wrote. "He waved haughtily to the cheer-
ing local children with their horrid little flags. Like Germanicus in his
chariot making a triumphal entry into Rome with his spoils."

I was watching a show. It wasn't real. It wasn't happening to me.

"I guess they *are* rounding up *all* the whites," said Alette, when more
vehicles with whites, including some Eurasians, were added to our
Palembang-bound caravan. Obviously we wouldn't be able to reach it in
one day. Women on my truck guessed our overnight stop would be Lahat,
which had a fair-sized hotel.

Every so often along the way all the vehicles stopped and the Japanese
who were driving them, or riding together in separate "escort" cars, tumbled
out, lined up, and relieved themselves. We prisoners in the trucks were not
given such an opportunity. Neither did the Japanese give us anything to eat
or drink, although they regularly stopped to eat food they had brought for
themselves.

In Lahat we were indeed all crammed into the Julianahotel, named
after Princess Juliana, daughter of Holland's queen. Men and women were
reunited, but had to sleep separately on the floors of rooms from which the
beds had been removed. Father came over to tell us he had had good
conversations with men on his truck about what the Dutch government
would do when the Japanese were ousted again. Mac asked me how to spell
the Malay word for *lekas*, which means quick. He had discovered, as I had,
that "lekas, lekas" were favorite words of the Japanese. Everything had to be
done quickly, even when there didn't seem to be the slightest reason for a
rush.

I don't recall how many people and how much luggage had to be
accommodated in the room where my sisters and I slept. I do remember that
a Japanese soldier brought a mat for everyone who didn't have a mattress to

sleep on. He hammered nails into the wall and fetched string to hang up mosquito nets. He consulted a Malay-Japanese dictionary every time he wished to say something. Since he started everything he said with "You people," which in Malay is *Kamu Orang*, everyone in the room called him Kamu Orang.

Kamu Orang used his bayonet to open cans of food for women who hadn't brought a can opener and fussed around among us women and children like a counselor in a summer camp. He gave us renewed hope that the situation might improve. There might again be consideration and understanding from the Japanese.

The next day there was none.

We were to ride a train from Lahat to Palembang, a distance of 160 kilometers, and were herded from the Julianahotel to the train station. The little group of 20 that left Krui two days before had grown to some 60 by the time we reached the Julianahotel, and now grew again as a procession of Dutch nuns in flowing white robes and more men, women, and children joined us at the Lahat station. All carried baskets, bundles, suitcases, bedding. At least they had some warning, I thought. Also among the newcomers was a group of *Poelau Dius* survivors, but no women and no one I knew.

Some of the people in the new group knew people in our group from the hotel, and the "Oh, you're here too," added a gay touch to the worried conversations about what would happen to us in Palembang.

When the train finally came, the Japanese soldiers sat in the two passenger cars while we were pushed into cattle vans with the doors tightly closed or onto an open tender behind the steam locomotive. It was on the latter that I huddled with my father and sisters under towels we had bought in one of the villages. Embers of glowing coal burned holes into the towels and smoke from the engine soon made us look like stokers. For the second day, the Japanese failed to feed us. At every station stop, however, local vendors crowded the platform, and sometimes our captors let us buy bananas, pineapples, or juicy oranges. But other times they shooed the vendors away with their bayonets, making raucous sounds. Sometimes one Japanese would ignore the vendor, let him sell us his stuff, and a minute later another Japanese would chase the vendor away. We were never going to have much luck at second-guessing our captors.

"Horses!" cried Antoinette, as she stepped off the tender onto the Palembang train station.

I looked over her head at the platform. Standing higgledy-piggledy beside it were a number of railroad cars that were being used as military barracks. Japanese soldiers were milling around dressed only in loin cloths. Their heads were shaven. And, yes, off the platform were horses. Horses in this area, which is nothing but rivers and marshes . . .

On the platform Japanese soldiers, with their clothes on, were trying to bring order to the flotsam of people streaming out of the cattle cars and the tender. Now we had to wait through another interminable process of separating the men from the women and children.

This time, all of us perceived that the separation might be longer than before. With a sinking feeling, I suddenly realized that we might be seeing the last of Father for an unknown period. Father—who had taken care of everything throughout these weeks, who had made suggestions and parlayed for us with those strange and sometimes terrifying Japanese men. I glanced at the men in loin cloths and shuddered.

Electric bulbs were dangling from wires that had been strung from car to car in the makeshift military encampment. The men looked Mongolian, and I had a vision of Genghis Khan and his Mongolians storming through Europe on horseback, swinging their sabers, plundering, murdering, burning out entire towns.

On the platform a man now hugged his wife and little girls, who let out heart-rending cries of "*Pappie.*" A woman opened a bundle and searched for a toy or for something to eat for a crying son. A man gave money to his wife, "Here you'd better take some." A wife said to a husband, "Here you should have a towel, too." The nuns strode around, trying to help mothers with children and to comfort those who obviously needed it. One of the *Poelau Bras* survivors distributed bananas among women who stood alone.

Father, who had been talking with some of these men, now walked over to us again and said, "The bridge over the Musi has been destroyed, so we all have to go across into the town by boat. Chins up," he said, and hugged each of us briefly. Then he walked back to where the men were assembling. They were then marched off into the darkness as women waved and sobbed. Some time later, we women, with the children, were told to move on. It appeared there was still room on the ferry across the river. The women would cross together with the men.

Naturally, on the ferry the men and women mixed again, and after the crossing a new separation was necessary: men on one side of the street, women and children on the other. This time the order to separate had come so quickly that we couldn't embrace Father again. But from the other side of the street he held up his hand, and with his fingers made a V sign, "Churchill's sign."

Men and women began shouting to each other across the empty street. Antoinette had just said to me, "You have the loudest voice, you tell Father not to worry about us," when a Japanese guard on our side became irritated, gave out a sound like a dog's howl, and slapped the faces of the women who had been shouting to the men.

Prisoners! We were prisoners. How hard it was to believe for our group of comfortable, upper-middle-class householders so used to going about and doing as we wished. But the slaps, the orders, the pointed bayonets all brought us up short.

For what seemed an eternity, but was probably no more than half an hour, each group stood silently on its side of the street. We were waiting, but waiting for what? The footsteps of the guards walking up and down sounded hollow and eerie.

"I wish they'd get on with their plans," a woman near me sighed. "This suspense is killing."

Other women spoke.

"The children should have been in bed ages ago."

"My little one has diarrhea, but I didn't bring a potty."

"Here, you can borrow mine."

Two women began discussing in low tones what they had chosen to grab up as they left home.

"How smart of you to bring kitchen stuff. We may have to do our own cooking."

"I also had my cook pack some of those white enamel eating bowls the servants use."

A stout, middle-aged woman dabbed her face with 4711 cologne.

"Oh, I hate this clammy climate. I've been six years on Sumatra and am still not used to it."

The smell of *eau de cologne* hung in the air briefly and reminded me of old ladies during Sunday services in the Dutch Reformed church I attended in The Hague with my grandparents. My last year in high school I had

The bayonets always looked razor sharp and the soldiers rarely looked friendly.
(Photo courtesy National Institute for War Documentation, Amsterdam)

stayed in their home because my parents were again living in the Netherlands East Indies. Prim and proper, the ladies sat each Sunday in the same pew. How far away was that protected and well-regulated world.

Antoinette nudged me. She lifted her head in the direction of the men. I saw Father walking up to a guard and pointing to my sisters and me. Apparently he had wheedled permission to talk to us. Stepping on his bandaged feet with a deliberate buoyancy, he crossed the street. We three moved to the edge of the sidewalk.

"The men are going to the Palembang jail," said Father, "and you are all going to a women's camp in Palembang."

Amazing! I thought. He should have been in intelligence. He always manages to turn up the necessary information. To me, he said, "Be sure you get a doctor to look at Antoinette's arm. She needs immediate treatment. The Japanese say this internment is only temporary. They want to sort us all out. Maybe the four of us will still be allowed to go back to Java." He walked back.

Did he really feel the optimism he expressed? I wonder now.

Soon the men were taken away on trucks, and the desolation of the darkened, empty street overtook us.

An older woman next to Antoinette sobbed, "What will they do to my husband? He's on a special diet."

"My father just assured us that the Japanese only want to sort us out," said Antoinette. "Your husband may be back home with you soon, and you'll be able to take care of him again."

Some of the women wanted to sit down, but the guard would have none of it. We had to remain standing. Some of the children fell asleep on bundles or in their mothers' arms.

Most of us were silent again, each left to her own thoughts and hopes. But one woman's voice boomed through the quiet the stubborn thought we all still shared.

"There must be a mistake, to capture women and children. Whoever heard of it? We'll be released soon, I'm sure."

As if the guard had understood her Dutch and wanted to make sure we knew who was in charge, he started to regroup us in lots of 20. He made this clear by four times pouncing his right hand into the air with out-stretched fingers.

I looked around. With whom should my sisters and I stand?

"What about the nuns?" whispered Antoinette.

"The nuns?" I asked, bewildered. I was raised in a Protestant family, had gone to a Protestant school, where I learned history from a Protestant viewpoint: during 300 years of Protestant-Catholic conflicts, the Catholics were always the villains. Still, the six nuns exuded calm and self-control—two qualities my parents had fostered in us. Why not the nuns? I thought.

I walked over to the oldest, whose white wimple framed a strong, wrinkled face straight out of a Renaissance painting.

"May my sisters and I stand with you?" I asked.

"Of course. I saw you girls at the Lahat station. I think you are as tall as our Sister Catharinia."

Antoinette, Alette, and I picked up our sarong bundles of village-bought belongings and the package of mosquito nets we had taken from the rest house and stood near the nuns. As I looked at the white habits and the friendly faces inside the wimples, I realized that I had never talked to a Catholic before, let alone a nun. But this war-imposed meeting in the

Sister Catharinia in Holland before leaving for Sumatra in 1938.

Palembang street was the beginning of life-long friendships.

With the nuns, three mothers and children, and a mountain of sarong bundles, wicker suitcases, cardboard boxes, one big capoc mattress, and bundles of pots and pans, my sisters and I made a 15-minute truck ride. The truck stopped before a barbed-wire barricade that crossed the asphalt street. Before a little wooden guardhouse stood yet another Japanese soldier with yet another bayonet mounted on a rifle.

Beyond the barricade I could see a row of red-tile-roofed white stucco houses built for European residents who had left Palembang just before the Japanese entered the city in mid-February. The houses were situated on both sides of a short street that ran along the crest of a little hill. An even shorter street angled down on the right.

Women emerged from the houses and moved slowly toward the gate. They were all much older than I, in their late twenties, thirties, or forties. Some already had snow-white hair. The group looked eerily ghostlike in the yellow light of the brightly shining street lamps. Some wore men's army shirts tucked into sarongs. Many were barefoot, and several had bandages around their hands.

More women collected near the gate, and children too. When they saw us, they cried loudly in Dutch, "*Nieuwe mensen, nieuwe mensen*," new people, new people.

Several of the women were speaking English. "How odd," I thought. "What are Englishwomen doing in Palembang?"

"Do you see what the streets are called?" Alette asked me.

"Yes, I saw." Signs marked them as Irenelaan and Bernhardlaan. Bernhard was the husband of Princess Juliana. Irene was the name of Juliana's daughter, born just a few weeks before the outbreak of the war. Newspapers reported that the princess had chosen the name because it means "peace."

"Ironic, isn't it? A concentration camp—because that's certainly what this place looks like—with a sign reading Irenelaan."

"Those reminders of our royal family won't stay up long," said Antoinette. "They'll soon be replaced by something in Japanese characters that none of us can read."

As my sisters and I were standing with our luggage near the truck, trying to get our bearings, a slight, peppy-looking woman with a Cockney accent said to me, "Counting your truck load, we are now 400 women and children. There are about a 140 of us from Singapore. We had homes there or in upstate Malaya. And we were all so grateful to find room in the evacuation ships that left Singapore just before the Japanese marched in. But three of our ships were bombed and sunk in the Bangka Straits—the *Vyner Brooke, Giang Bee, Kuala*—and one was captured—the *Mata Hari*. In getting off the *Vyner Brooke* some of us slid down ropes and burned the skin off our hands."

That explained the bandages.

Other women chimed in with information. During the bombings many lives were lost. Survivors spent grueling hours in boats, on rafts, hanging onto orange crates, and some even swam for days. Near the *Vyner Brooke*, the sea was covered with oil. Swimmers' clothes had become saturated with it. When they reached the shore of Bangka Island, local people had given them sarongs. And British military men imprisoned nearby were able to supply the women with shirts.

So it was shipwrecks that accounted for the bizarre costumes, I thought. For the first time, the enormity of suffering that this war was causing overwhelmed me.

The war had already raged for two years in Europe, but to us it had been a distant drama, an abstract event to read about in newspapers. I had had fun helping to raise funds for the Spitfires Churchill needed, and taking the Red Cross first aid course on Tarakan. When the war came closer and engulfed the island of Tarakan, it became a story told to us by Father after his escape. Next, war casualties became coded messages in the Batavia office where I worked, when, in an attempt to turn the Japanese invasion fleet away from Java, most of the Allied Navy was lost in the Java Sea. Still, the war had not really touched me.

The war couldn't have come closer than it did when enemy bombers attacked the *Poelau Bras* and half the people aboard perished. But the sinking of the *Poelau Bras* seemed an isolated, freakish incident. Once the ordeal of the lifeboat was over, the three weeks' trek through the Sumatra jungles—despite bloodsucker infections and the fear of not being able to find an escape boat—had provided a sense of adventure. We were going to get away yet!

Now I was *surrounded* by war victims, women and children uprooted from their homes, some washed up on foreign shores.

"Where are we going to put you up?" cried one of the women at the gate. "These are five-room bungalows, built for single people or couples with one or two children. Thirty people live in ours. What are we going to do with you? All our space is filled up with bodies, bedding, and belongings."

"Oh, but our house is not cluttered with belongings," said someone with an Australian accent. She turned out to be an Australian Army nurse, one of 32 in the camp. "We were all on the *Vyner Brooke* and arrived here with nothing except the clothes on our backs. Some of the Dutch women gave us things, bless 'em, but we still have nothing to sit on, no tables either, no beds. After the Dutch departed, locals must have looted the houses, for there's hardly any furniture left. And, of course, we have no suitcases full of clothes or cooking equipment, as some Dutch people here have."

It was like a chorus. These women couldn't wait to initiate us into our new life.

A group of sisters of the Royal Australian Army Nursing Service in their working uniforms of grey dress, red cape, white veil, and brown shoes. Another group of 65 nurses left Singapore on the *Vyner Brooke*. Twelve lost their lives when the Japanese sunk the ship, 21 were massacred on a beach they swam to, and eight would die in the camp.

"Yes, nothing at all to cook on. But we made a stove with bricks pried from a wall. And we're burning up doors for fuel."

"No fuel has come in yet," said another woman.

Judging by her accent, I thought she must also be an Australian Army nurse.

"You newcomers had better brace yourselves for eating rice. That's all we get. No bread at all . . ."

"At least we can drink the tap water," said someone else.

"Yeah . . . when the tap actually works. Nothing works here. The electricity is off most of the time, so those electric ranges in the kitchens are useless. I can't imagine why the street lights are on now. Probably to make it easier for the guards to count you. These chaps love to count us, but it always takes a while, because they get mixed up."

Women stepped forward to offer space.

"Our house could take five. Mind you, we don't have ritzy accommodations, but you can't sleep on the street. We may have another of those torrential monsoon rains."

"Four is O.K. in our house. But, please, no children."

"Who do you think will want to have us?" muttered Antoinette.

Just then a familiar-looking woman came running up the hill. "Hey, Colijn girls!" she cried. "I heard you were on the last truck. I was on the *Poelau Bras* too, with my husband."

I remembered seeing her with her husband on the ship. I wondered whether I should ask about the husband, but before I decided on the right thing to say, she told us.

"Yesterday the Japanese showed me a list of names of all the survivors accounted for so far in the three lifeboats that made land, but Joop's name wasn't on it."

"Maybe a fourth lifeboat has landed somewhere else, or maybe one of the rafts made it ashore." But I knew as well as she did that only three lifeboats were launched. The others had been blasted by the bombs, and no one on the ship had given the rafts a chance. I was thinking hard what to say next that could be comforting to her, but her nervous chatter didn't stop.

"Do you remember the woman with the ten-day-old baby, the one who came aboard in her housecoat right from the hospital? She's here, too. With the baby, who survived the lifeboat voyage on her mother's milk, and with her six-year-old. With you three, that makes seven of us *Poelau Bras* survivors in camp. You girls must have had a long day. It's almost midnight. *Our* time, that is. I don't go for all this nonsense of living by Nippon time. I still have my watch, it's working, and I keep it at our time.

"Why don't you girls come with me? You can spend tonight in my room. There isn't a centimeter of space left on the floor, but I can move my things about a bit. I don't have much, and I'm sure Mrs. de Bert and her four children, my temporary roommates, won't mind doing the same. I'll help them stack up some of their stuff."

The four youngsters remained asleep as their mother and Mrs. van den Hout stacked and shoved, pushed and pulled, to clear space on the tile floor for the three of us to sleep.

Mrs. van den Hout loaned us sofa pillows she had found in the garden—"The looters must have thrown them there"—and helped us string our two nets.

So began my first night in the internment camp. I felt momentarily safe, fussed over by a kindly woman. No Japanese were in sight to give orders. My sisters and I were together. We knew where Father was. Though a prisoner, at least he was in the same town. We would no doubt meet him again soon, when all this madness was straightened out. Only Mother's fate was nagging. Where was she? Was she in a camp like this? Was she being treated well?

Antoinette, Alette, and I fell asleep—lying on bright green pillows with a pattern of red hibiscus. It was a tiny island of warmth in a dark, war-torn world. And we still hadn't gotten it through our heads that we three upstanding citizens—young women with dreams and plans—were in the camp of an occupying enemy.

No mistake had been made. We were prisoners of the Japanese.

Cooking facilities in our first camp were as makeshift as shown in a camp on Java. (Photo courtesy Museon, The Hague)

Chapter Six

Houses Camp:
Roll Call

As soon as we had crawled out from under our mosquito nets early the next morning, Mrs. van den Hout, already up and dressed, whispered, "I'll make us oatmeal porridge for breakfast.

"Someone gave me a brazier she found in the back quarters of the house she now lives in. Probably left there by the servants. I never cooked on a brazier in my life, but I'm already getting used to it. It's outside on the veranda. One of the Aussies gave me wood to burn in it."

"What kind of food do they give us?" I asked.

"I've only been here three days, so I don't really know. A food ration was delivered by truck yesterday. The driver, a local man, dumped it all on the street. Rice in a gunny sack and some rotten vegetables called *kangkung*, a kind of overaged spinach. Not the potatoes we asked for, nor the bread.

"Oh, we did get a ration of duck eggs, too. It worked out to one egg for seven people."

"How do you divide one egg among seven people?"

"Some used the egg in a soup, or hard-boiled it, mashed it, and gave everyone a speck, or scrambled it with lots of water and gave everyone a teaspoonful. Some drew lots."

"What did you decide upon?" asked Alette.

"I'll have to wait for my turn. The few eggs for this house went to other *kongsis*."

My sisters and I had been in the Dutch East Indies long enough to know that the Chinese word kongsi was used for company, partnership, or group. Here the word was apparently used for cooking groups.

Mrs. van den Hout continued. "The largest kongsi is the Australian nurses, all 32 of them crammed into one of the houses on Irenelaan. There are also British, Dutch, Dutch Eurasian, and English Eurasian kongsi's."

I later would reflect that these were not segregations of racism. They came more out of the need for comfort. It was reassuring to be with one's own kind in a life so suddenly and drastically changed.

"The smallest kongsi is of one like me. I couldn't decide who to join. But if you girls would like to team up with me, I'd be delighted."

We looked at each other and nodded assent.

She beamed, "Good."

And that's how my sisters and I started life in a kongsi of four in what we later called the "houses camp."

After generous portions of Mrs. van den Hout's Quaker Oats, which she cooked in an empty tin, the three of us walked up the hill of Bernhardlaan to see what was going on in the camp. The coolness of the morning had gone, and the air was already humid and heavy.

"Maybe we can find out why we are here," said Antoinette.

No one knew for sure. Sister Catharinia, of the nuns we had joined at the Palembang street the night before, said she had heard that a Japanese officer had told someone that we were here to be protected against the local population. Now why would they turn against us? she wondered.

Betty Jeffrey, one of the Australian nurses we met later that morning, said she had heard that Japan had plans for a Greater East Asia Co-Prosperity Sphere in which there was no room for non-Asians.

"That's what the American journalist in our lifeboat said," I added.

"Anyway, it is against all international conventions to intern us Army nurses."

"They also interned our mother," said Alette. "She was working as a

Red Cross nurse on Tarakan."

An English woman who introduced herself as Shelagh Brown joined us. She lived in a small garage of house number 9 with her mother and a dozen other people, "packed like the proverbial sardines." She looked five or six years older than I. Other women from her garage sauntered over, and we continued to vent our indignation at being in this terrible place.

Betty Jeffrey in 1941 in her outdoor uniform just before leaving Australia for Malaya.

"Well," someone said, "let's hope they'll soon see how silly this all is. Four hundred innocent women and children behind barbed wire. Sleeping on the floor. No mosquito nets, dreadful food . . ."

"And no shoes or clothes for the shipwrecked ones," chimed in another.

"Separated from our men . . ."

"What have we done to deserve all this? Especially those nice Dutch nuns, who spent their lives teaching, and the devoted missionaries from Singapore . . ."

"Housewives who were only taking care of children and husbands. No one here is actively engaged in the waging of war."

We noticed a small crowd gathering by the gate, and we walked over to see what was happening. The guard opened the gate and one of the women walked out from behind the barbed wire, free.

"Lucky girl," said Shelagh. "She's from Switzerland. Neutral country. And German nationals may leave, too, since Germany is an ally of Japan. I heard the Dutch Eurasians are given a choice, because of their part-Asian blood. But without husbands to take care of them . . . Look, there's Nel."

Nel Mahodim, a Dutch Eurasian, was trying to communicate with the guard. It looked like she, too, could go. We stared in amazement as she turned and walked back into the camp. The women gathered around her and asked, "Why didn't you go?"

Nel responded shyly and softly, "I feel safer here than outside with all those strange soldiers about."

A silence fell on the little group. We had all heard dreadful stories of Japanese soldiers pillaging and raping.

Shelagh was eager to change the subject. "One of the missionaries in our garage has written 'The Palembang Camp Song.' It's to be sung to the tune of 'A Hunting We Will Go.'" May I read the last verse to you?" She pulled a note from the much-too-big man's shirt she had been given after her shipwreck.

> *The sun sinks low, the darkness falls,*
> *The mosquitoes leave their lairs.*
> *We shift our table, spread our rugs,*
> *Each one a special couch prepares.*
> *If netless, armed for the fight*
> *She to the floor repairs.*
> *So, a-sleeping we will go.*
> *A-sleeping we will go, will go.*
> *Our foes our spirits cannot quell,*
> *A-sleeping we will go.*

She had just read the last line when a guard blew a piercing whistle and galvanized the camp for *tenko* or roll call. Women poured out of the houses. Women filled the streets. Like a river of flowing lava, everyone moved toward the guardhouse.

"Oh dear, we have to be counted again and go through the bowing routine," said Shelagh. "And it is already so hot. I think they wait on purpose, so we can suffer in the sun."

"You mean we have to bow to the guard?" asked Alette.

"No, no, to the emperor of Japan. The guard merely personifies him. That's why he's so fussy that we do it right. A smirk on your face, a wrong angle, a gesture that might be interpreted as a slight to Hirohito, Emperor of the Land of the Rising Sun, upsets him. You may wind up with a resound-

Bowing to the Emperor was mandatory in all Japanese prison camps in Southeast Asia. (Photo courtesy National Institute for War Documentation, Amsterdam)

ing slap on your face or a vicious kick to the shin. Two days ago, we all had to stand an interminable time, stand in the sun, because one poor soul had not bowed properly.

"Stupid, that counting. As if we would run away. Where would we white women hide on this island with a dark-skinned population? How could we get off? But we'd better join the crowd and go through the circus."

My sisters and I followed Shelagh and sought out Mrs. van den Hout. We had to be counted house by house. At the beginning of Irenelaan, where the counting took place, I saw for the first time how many children there were in the camp—mostly Dutch, babes in arms, toddlers clinging to mothers' hands, grade-school-aged children.

Near the gate stood the guard, a crude-looking creature wearing the already familiar khaki cap with flap in the back and carrying one of those ugly bayonets on his rifle. In front of him the "houses" formed lines. A Dutch woman I had not seen before had volunteered to be captain of house number 16. Later I learned she was Mrs. van Zanen, who would give me a pair of shoes.

"*Keirei!*" hollered the guard.

Apparently this word meant "Bow," because everyone jackknifed from the waist down, head low, arms held perpendicularly to the body. My sisters and I did the same.

"Absurd business," I muttered to Alette next to me.

"Shhh," hissed Mrs. van den Hout.

The house captains called out in Malay how many of their house were present. The guard checked the number against a sheet he had brought along in his uniform pocket, leaving his weapon propped against the barbed wire gate.

"Thank goodness, tenko went off without a hitch today," said our new room neighbor, Mrs. de Bert, as we returned to house number 16. "Two days ago we all had to stand in the sun, even the children. One woman fainted, but after she came to, she had to stand again. One of the Eurasians who speaks Malay fluently uses a Malay verb for this practice, *jemur*, dry in the sun. We were being jemured, a very telling expression I think."

Tenko would become a daily exercise. Some women hated it for the duration of internment. Such humiliation to have to bow to this unknown man in Tokyo. We had never even seen a photo of him. But others played mind games, telling themselves they were bowing to God, to Jesus, to a beloved person, or to a different person every day. One of the women of garage number 9 chose from her list of favorite classical composers. "No Japanese can control our minds," she said.

At first I found it difficult to distance myself from the real situation. The guard and his odious whistle were a constant reminder of captivity. But I, too, learned to bow to the emperor without giving *him* a thought.

As days went by, the fear of being raped would diminish. Early on, Japanese officers tried to recruit some of the Australians to entertain them at a club. The sisters successfully thwarted the effort by all looking as ugly as they could and saying no to all overtures. In our camp no one was raped. We developed a theory that the Japanese didn't like our smell. It appears that the soldiers had been strictly forbidden to sexually molest the imprisoned women. Such an order was not uniformly followed in all the camps, but if a soldier was caught disobeying this order, he was usually executed for the offense.

On the other hand, in a few camps on Java the Japanese officers had young women dragged out of the internment camp to live in a bordello and forced them to satisfy the men's sexual needs. Since rape, and repeated rape, is not something women like to talk about, the "comfort girls" kept the story to themselves. But in recent years they have begun to talk and write books. Jane Ruff O'Herne, a Dutch woman who emigrated to Australia after the war, wrote *Fifty Years of Silence* which was turned into a documentary by an Australian filmmaker, "a beautifully made film, a most moving and brave document," said my daughter in Amsterdam who saw it on Dutch television.

That first day in camp my sisters and I easily put the idea of rape aside. Surely we wouldn't have to stay around these brutes for very long.

"I'm sure the Red Cross will do something about us soon," I said that evening, as the three of us sat outside number 16.

"I guess we'll soon hear from Father. I understand the jail is only a few kilometers away," Antoinette said.

Alette's thoughts were in Borneo. "What do you think Mother is doing right now? Her second time of being interned."

During the Boer War in South Africa (1899-1902), my maternal grandmother and her five children were herded into a chicken coop while British soldiers set their farm afire. My grandfather, who had left Holland to become a farmer in the Transvaal, was away on his best horse fighting the "Rednecks." When nothing but two walls of the farm were standing, the soldiers carted the family off to a concentration camp for women and children. Mother was then nine years old.

"Don't you think it's ironic that the idea of a concentration camp for women and children was first dreamt up by the English Lord Kitchener," I thought aloud. "Now the Japanese are putting English women and children in a Kitchener-style camp."

"Don't mention it here," Alette suggested.

✥ ✥ ✥

Three months later we were still there. No more people left the camp. No more new people arrived. No news from the outside world arrived either, which created a terrible sense of isolation. What was going on in the war? Where were the husbands who had gone to war? Were they still alive and prisoners of war? And how were our men in the Palembang jail? Several Dutch women had husbands there, some of the British women, too. And

87

our father was there. We were not allowed to send or receive messages.

"So close," fumed Antoinette. "Only a few kilometers away, and not yet a word. And the Bible says love thy enemy!"

When it became clear that release was not imminent, the camp settled down. We began creating a semblance of order, a semblance of the previous life.

There had been no official way to ask for anything. Individual women had just trotted up to the guardhouse and asked for what they needed. Soon the guards tired of the stream of complaints and refused to talk with anyone but camp representatives.

It took some doing to agree upon a representative everyone in this mixed camp could be happy with. We finally appointed two: On behalf of the Dutch, the Reverend Mother Laurentia; and Jean McDowell, a physician who had practiced in Singapore, on behalf of *de Engelsen*. They were the British and Australians, whom we Dutch, lazily and incorrectly, of course, lumped together as "the English," a habit we kept up all through our incarceration.

Some of the Dutch Protestants were troubled to have a Catholic representative, but there wasn't anyone else with quite the same dignity, poise, and supposed wisdom as this superior of the Sisters of Carolus Borromeus of Lahat.

The pair always went to the guardhouse in tandem. Tall Mother Laurentia walked with long, purposeful steps and a look of determination on her gentle, handsome face. She wore a blue work dress made for her by one of the sisters from a bolt of cotton fabric Mother Laurentia had providentially brought along. This habit was far less confining and figure-concealing than her original white one, and the looser-fitting veil soon showed some of her greying hair. Mother Laurentia had decided that the shaving of nuns' heads was not necessary anymore.

Next to her, Dr. McDowell—in a red skirt with white polka dots and a short-sleeved white blouse that became grubbier with every washing—looked like a school girl. But the curls cascading down her temples were grey. She wore the one stethoscope the camp owned, hoping that her medical status would add clout to her pleas for better accommodations, clothing, food, and medicines.

The two women spoke to the guard in Malay or English. Sometimes

Tine Muller, the mother with the infant from the *Poelau Bras,* went along to translate. Having lived in Japan when her Dutch naval officer husband was attached to the Dutch embassy there, she had learned some Japanese. Whether the guard understood the request or not made little difference. The answer was likely to be no, even when we asked for quinine pills for those who had come down with malaria from the anopheles mosquito. "What can you expect, no mosquito nets to sleep under," we said to each other. However, many with nets also contracted malaria, a debilitating disease of regularly recurring bouts of chills, followed by high fevers.

A "Red Cross Committee" made the decisions about which mothers should receive a share of the few cans of milk the Japanese once in a while sent in. It also deliberated which "camp poor" should share in the money raised at a charity bazaar—where a hat made from a woven-grass bag was raffled off and "needlebooks" were sold. These were small, rectangular pieces of cloth sewn together like a book, usually with a cover of finely embroidered rice-sacking, to hold needles.

When the Japanese sent in a bolt of black cloth to be used to black out the windows, the Red Cross Committee divided it among the houses. No one screened off the windows, however. We preferred to sit in the dark, letting the air come in. We used the black material for clothes.

Many of us needed money. Most of the shipwrecked had none. With money we could buy food or utensils from fellow prisoners or from an Indian vendor. He was sporadically allowed to come to the camp with his oxcart bringing such needed items as needles, soap, tooth brushes, and treats like *gula jawa,* sugar made from the sap of the sugar palm and sold as round cakes wrapped in banana leaves.

Even though money could not yet make the difference between life and death, women without it were racking their brains for ways of earning it off women with money. Shelagh's mother made hats out of the woven-grass bags the vegetables were occasionally delivered in. Australian nurses in Betty Jeffrey's house gave haircuts. Some women made cookies to sell.

There had been talk in the camp about pooling money and spending it on the community as a whole. This, I found out later, was done in some of the POW camps. In our women's camp the idea didn't get off the ground. "My husband gave me money to take care of the children," said a Dutch mother, "so that's who I'll spend the money on."

Father had given my sisters and me money. I also had my three months' severance pay. Wrapped in oil cloth, it hadn't gotten so wet after the shipwreck that I couldn't dry out the bills upon reaching land. Why should we three now put money in a pool?

We set up other semblances of our previous life, such as a library for adults, singing groups, and school for the children. At one count, we had a total of 92 children in the camp. For the Dutch children, lessons were organized by the Sisters of Carolus Borromeus and the Sisters of The Sacred Heart, who had taught school in Palembang. Without textbooks of any kind, the Blue Sisters and the Striped Sisters, as they were often called in reference to their habits, sat surrounded by young pupils on the ground outside if it didn't rain or on some sheltered veranda if it did. The nuns taught reading from a hand-written reader, and writing and arithmetic on paper from precious copybooks they had brought into the camp. The older children learned to memorize Dutch history and the names of the capitals of the eleven Dutch provinces.

When we arrived in the camp we found books strewn all over the houses, evidently not of interest to the looters, who had taken virtually everything else the former Dutch residents had had to leave behind. There were Dutch novels and a few English novels, like *Gone With the Wind* and *Anthony Adverse*, and one French novel, Victor Hugo's hefty tome, *Les Misérables*. Sister Catharinia used it to teach high-school French to Alette.

The books wound up in a large box marked CAMP LIBRARY. It was shunted from here to there until it wound up on the covered walkway in front of the second place my sisters and I lived. I became the camp librarian, with posted library hours. It was a blessing that the books were designated library books early in our internment. Had they been left without a label, their pages would surely have been used to light fires in the many braziers and fireplaces that were constantly sputtering in the camp.

Mother Laurentia conducted a choir for Dutch children and one for Dutch adults. The "English" had a church choir as well as a glee club, which later became the Camp Choral Society.

The English groups usually were conducted by Miss Dryburgh, one of the four Presbyterian missionaries, or by Norah Chambers, a British woman who had studied violin, piano, and singing at the Royal Academy of Music in London. There were no songbooks in the camp, except for a *Presbyte-*

Margaret Dryburgh (third from left), and
three other Presbyterian missionaries.

rian Church Hymnery, the ancient and modern hymns of the Church of
England, and perhaps a Dutch song book or two that have gone unre-
corded. Most songs were sung from memory.

Antoinette and Alette, who spoke good English, joined the English
choirs. They copied the words of songs into some of the copy books we had
found (by a not yet appreciated stroke of good luck) in a closet of house
number 16.

I often was envious of Antoinette and Alette, and wished I could join
them. They were different girls when they had been singing. They were
buoyed up, happier. But I was that *brommertje*, the unmusical "little buzzer"
of the third grade who had had to stay behind in the classroom with a few other
brommertjes and sing traditional Dutch folk tunes when the rest of the class
went to the school gym to sing in harmony with a real singing teacher.

A choir was sometimes accompanied by someone in the Australian
house, playing a battered piano that had long lost its pitch through expo-
sure to tropical humidity and lack of tuning.

A Dutch Salvation Army woman had been able to bring a small
harmonium into the camp, and she offered her portable instrument for

evenings of entertainment. However, the harmonium's principal role in the camp was in Dutch Protestant church services, and orthodox church members protested that it would be a desecration of a religious instrument to use it for worldly music—or, worse, to accompany the dance troupe in which women kicked up their legs in rehearsal for a variety show the singers were planning to put on. Such dancing, the church members held, was immoral.

Both sides in the argument stood their ground. But even the observation that our women were showing their bare legs only to other women, and *not* with the aim to excite men, failed to convince the very small contra-harmonium-for-glee-club group. The owner of the harmonium settled the matter by saying, as if she were talking to squabbling six-year-olds, "If you fight about this harmonium, no one can have it."

"A tempest in a tea cup," said Alette. "That harmonium isn't so melodious any more, either. So what's the fuss about?"

Everyone was sorry when the dispute was over. It had been a marvelous topic of conversation on Irenelaan where we strolled in the evening, and in little gossiping clusters in the houses.

The troupe danced to the tunes of the hoarse piano in a program of vocal numbers sung a cappella—full English choir, full Dutch choir, solos, duets, part songs—and a monologue and skits. For these Miss Dryburgh wrote the text.

♫   ♫   ♫

The Japanese had ordered that house number 16 and two others be vacated, and the residents spread out over the remaining 13. My sisters and I said good-bye to kind-hearted Mrs. van den Hout and moved into a tiny cubicle in the servants' quarters of house number 13, probably once used as an ironing room. We called it our little Walhalla. We were now a kongsi of three.

One of us slept on the concrete counter along the rear wall. The two others slept on the concrete floor below. We had cut our two mosquito nets down to three and made mattress pads from gunny rice sacks filled with dry grass. The cubicle had no window. Light and air came in through the door opening. In rainy weather it was damp and clammy, and it had a

Basic household items: bag for storing belongings, fan for flapping fires, coconut shell to use for eating and drinking.

permanent musty, mildewy smell. It did afford privacy, except when the 30 people in the house were lined up next to the cubicle for the bathroom.

This was an Eastern-style bathroom for bathing. It had a water tank in the corner. We would have plunged a dipper into the tank and thrown water over ourselves to wash, had there been water in the tank. Instead, each woman had to bring her own water in a bucket, filled from a central tap that might be running, or from the rain spout. In those days we all observed prewar criteria of modesty and considered it important to take turns bathing behind closed doors.

My sisters and I took turns cooking in tins on a donated brazier. We had never had to cook before but Mrs. van den Hout gave us tips, and cooking our daily rations of rice and vegetables did not require great culinary talents. Our girl scout experience came in handy. I found it rather restful to hunker down in front of the brazier and flap at the fire with our small bamboo fan—*if* the wood ration had not again been green and sappy and burnt only fitfully in clouds of acrid smoke.

Occasionally the camp was treated to a ration of coconuts. One of the Eurasian women showed us how to make the best use of a coconut. Pull the shaggy outer husk off, and you can use it for a pot scrubber or toothbrush. Tie fronds together, and you have a broom. Bash the hard coconut shell in half and, after prying the meat out, you have two bowls. You can eat the meat as candy, or grate it and squeeze it and you get "coconut milk." This can be used for a sauce made, for example, with ginger root or tamarind. These native condiments, for sale from the Indian vendor, had to be ground in a granite mortar with a granite pestle we borrowed.

We three signed up when women were asked to volunteer for community jobs, such as street sweeping or doling out the food rations. The latter was one of the more taxing jobs, because the truck always arrived in the hottest part of the day. This did not prevent fellow-internees from gathering around the truck to make sure everyone received her fair share in the line-up of containers on the street. Thirty-two portions of raw rice in the tub for the Australian nurses . . . 15 in the pail for the kongsi of garage number 9 . . . five in the chamber pot of a Dutch family . . . three in the tin for the Colijn girls. Especially interested were the kibitzers when rare rations of *kacang hijau*—green, lentil-sized peas, great for vitamin B—had to be doled out, or when red chili peppers—great for vitamin C and good for making *sambal*—arrived.

In the evening women walked up and down short Irenelaan (four houses on each side), back and forth, back and forth, like tigers in a cage. That was the time when we told each other the latest rumors.

They were often too fantastic for even the most gullible internee to swallow: "The Allies are about to retake Sumatra," or "A Red Cross delegation will be visiting the camp next week." Still, such rumors brought hope. Occasionally a rumor had a real ring of truth to it. President Roosevelt's alleged statement that the troops would be home for Christmas—in other words, that the war would be over by Christmas—sustained all of us for many months in the houses camp.

Chapter Seven

The Captives' Hymn

Our camp was the responsibility of a succession of Japanese officers in well-pressed uniforms and tall polished boots. We often did not see our camp commander for weeks. He probably hates the sight of us, we figured, the reason for his being stuck on this dull outpost on Sumatra, far from the glory of military action.

The Japanese we did see and have to deal with daily were generally uneducated, uncouth, unkempt common soldiers. They were the men who counted us, ignored all of our requests, and occasionally treated us to their vile tempers.

The guards were particularly nasty when filled with rice wine. Then they would explode into a rage because a woman had the audacity to take a crate off the food truck to be used as a seat. Or because she was not properly dressed in anticipation of an officer's camp inspection. (Of course, she could only appear wearing the skimpy camp uniform of shorts and suntop because the plea for material had been ignored.) Or the guards would tear through one of the houses, ripping mattress pads, emptying suitcases and storage bags, in search of forbidden diaries.

95

But one day a guard strolled over to a house where some Australian women were entertaining and made signs at the window that he wanted to be invited in. No one in the house wanted him inside. He was offered a seat on the dustbin, raised for his benefit to window-level, and from there he watched the women. He was thoroughly amused and laughed hard at a pantomime two women put on.

Another guard asked the same women (in July) to sing "Auld Lang Syne" for him. They did, and he politely said "*Arigato,*" Japanese for "thank you."

But always, just when we began thinking that the Japanese might not be so bad after all, an awful thing would happen.

Behind the Australians' house the usual "black market" exchange was going on. A Chinese fellow was caught in the act of throwing a loaf of bread over the barbed-wire fence. The guards dragged him into the camp and tied him to a pole. They raised his arms above his head and tied a rope to his hands and neck in such a way that it would strangle him when he lowered his arms.

Mother Laurentia begged the guards to take him away, to no avail. We were not to help him in any way. One of the English boys defied the order and gave the man some water. During the night, someone put a knotted handkerchief over the man's head. The next morning, when the guard saw it, he yanked it off. It took three days for the man to die. This cruel spectacle was particularly hard on the children, who had to walk by the man on the way to *tenko.*

We had barely recovered from this shocking event when the mothers were told to send their eleven- and twelve-year-old sons to the guardhouse. The nine boys cast worried glances backward as they trooped away. Their fearful mothers wondered if their sons would return.

They did. But only briefly. "We have to be ready at four o'clock. We are being sent to a men's camp."

Pandemonium. "Which camp? Where?"

"We do not know."

One of the boys, Theo Rottier, recently related what happened:

"We had to walk through a corridor into a backyard, a walled backyard—a perfect scene for an execution. They ordered us to undress. One of the boys whispered, 'Hey, we're not going to do that!' The Japanese overheard him. After a few slaps and a few kicks, we were out of our pants in no

Theo Rottier (on left) with his mother and two brothers, a few years before internment.

time. And there we stood, naked, and they looked at us. They said, 'You, you, you . . . report at four o'clock with your personal belongings."

In vain, the mothers argued that their sons were still children and better off with their mothers. The Japanese retorted, "They are now men! They will go to a men's camp!"

The boys marched behind the guard out of the camp, trying to hide their fear. They had no idea where they were going. The mothers put up a brave front, too. But after the boys were gone, they cried.

It was many weeks before we heard that the boys had been sent to our men in the Palembang jail. Some boys found their fathers there; some knew no one at all, and were assigned a camp "uncle."

Throughout our internment, the Japanese remained impossible to fathom or understand. Even Tine, who had lived in Japan, admitted she couldn't "read" them.

I have since wondered whether a mediator fluent in Japanese and knowledgeable about our very different cultures could have improved the women's lot by creating mutual understanding. As it was, we thought the Japanese were totally alien creatures, and we must have seemed equally alien to them. What a change we were from the stereotypical Japanese woman, so submissive, obedient, and patient. We argued with the guards and complained endlessly. In the Japanese culture, I later learned, complaining about discomfort is bad manners.

In the years before the war the Japanese had been firmly indoctrinated with the idea that the Japanese spirit can conquer anything—fatigue, hunger, and enemy cannons. And here were we whites, who had lost the war, and we had the bad manners to make extravagant demands for furniture and food. Why, the Japanese themselves didn't have many comforts in their homeland. We must have matched perfectly their notion of luxury-oriented Westerners, making a big noise whenever they were displeased.

I don't think that many of us were aware—I certainly wasn't—of how inferior we must have appeared to the Japanese for these reasons. Besides, we had let ourselves be taken prisoner. The Japanese had nothing but contempt for soldiers who let themselves be captured. In the past such men returning to Japan had actually been executed or ostracized from the community. Suicide was often their only honorable way out. We women were not soldiers, and had nothing to do with the warfare, but . . . we were still women, low on the Japanese social totem pole.

One day, a guard drove a truck into the camp, looking very pleased with himself. He brought us a heavy, six-foot wooden pole for a "pestle" and a round block, two feet across and hollowed out, for a "mortar."

"This is to make your life easier," he managed to communicate to the bystanders. We would have to heave the pole up and down to pound rice, as I had seen women do in villages on Java. I had even taken pictures of them. So picturesque, those women in colorful sarongs and tight-fitting tops, often working in pairs and chanting as they raised and lowered the pole with unvarying rhythm, up and down . . . Of us three, Antoinette became the best pounder, with her characteristic persistence.

The block was stationed at the end of Irenelaan. I had gone up to watch Antoinette, who was pounding our ration of hard, dollar-sized slices of dried cassava called *gaplék*. Her brief black shorts, cut down from the pedal pushers she had received after the shipwreck, her little red-checkered suntop made from a dishtowel, and her bare arms, legs, and feet were already velvety from the dust of the flour.

"Why don't you stop? You can't pulverize those nasty last bits," I suggested.

"I'm sure I can get more flour yet. Besides, pounding helps me get rid of frustration. Think of it, already six months in this camp . . ." and she went on pounding faster and harder.

Finally she gave up, and with an empty Quaker Oats tin scooped the flour and residue out of the block onto a borrowed winnow about as large as a bicycle wheel. Holding the winnow with both hands, she shook it, until a hillock of flour lay on one side of the winnow and the residue on the other. Then she slid the flour into the tin and tossed the residue at the side of the street. "Tonight it's *ongel-ongel* for dinner, Helen." Ongel-ongel was the name we used for a porridge made of this flour and water. It had a slimy, glue-like consistency and tasted as awful as it sounded.

"No, you won't have to eat ongel-ongel," said Alette, who had just joined Antoinette and me at the block. "I made some bread."

Bread in the camp was a concoction cooked in a double boiler made from a Quaker Oats tin and a powdered milk tin. "I used the rice flour I pounded for us a few days ago."

"How is Baby Wim today?" I asked. Alette was carrying him in her arms.

"He's getting heavy, already four months old."

Wim Wenning was one of six babies born in the camp. His mother was an artist, and she did not mother well. Alette was passing through house number 13 one day and noticed that he had a dirty diaper. He was alone, his mother nowhere in sight. Alette located her, received a clean diaper, changed the baby, and washed the dirty diaper. The mother was delighted. Before long Alette did all the baby's laundry, fed him, and often entertained him when his mother was off working on her art projects.

I had been surprised to see this side of Alette. But then, I did not really know her well because of separations in our family. For example, for three years she lived with Father and Mother in an outpost on Borneo, Mother teaching her the first three years of grade school with a correspondence course, while Antoinette and I lived with a Dutch family in The Hague and went to schools there. As I discussed this maternal side of "our little sister" with Antoinette, she recalled how Alette took care of her pets on Borneo. Mother sent us photos of Alette feeding ducks, miniature deer or exotic birds or pushing Beppo in a stroller. Beppo was a baby orangutan. He had been found in the jungle after a hunter had shot his mother. When Mother took Alette back to Holland, Beppo was shipped to a zoo in The Hague. A spacious cage awaited him, where Alette would go and visit. The still small orangutan with the mahogany-colored hair and the girl with the blond locks hugged each other while zoo visitors outside the cage "oohed" and "aahed."

I asked Alette one day in the camp why she spent so much time on someone else's baby. She answered, "He's cute. And when I can help his mother, she can spend more time on the camp newspaper. That way, I indirectly contribute to the newspaper."

There was an English and a Dutch edition, typed with carbon copies on the camp's rickety typewriter and issued to each house. I still have a copy of the introductory issue, dated August 16, 1942. The masthead showed that the staff of six was equally divided between the "English" and the Dutch. The opening editorial read:

> We have the pleasure in starting a new periodical on its career and trust it will receive a welcome. Although we are not a large community, it is surprising how little we know about each other, and we hope that by sharing a common news bulletin we may help to strengthen the bonds between us by getting to know each other. "United we stand, divided we fall" is a saying that has proved true only too frequently of late. We trust that we shall learn to weld ourselves into a common loyalty and aim, sharing each other's joys and troubles and working for a common purpose . . . So this little paper joins the ranks of the newly born in the camp. May its career be successful, though none of us wishes it will be long.

"Church Notices" mentioned services in English and Dutch, Sunday schools, Bible studies. "Medical Notices" urged the pounding of egg shells (if we ever got an egg again) to create calcium powder for daily intake. This column warned, "There are many tropical sores in the camp. These are caused by dirty flies and mosquitoes which settle on every small scratch of the body. The flies and mosquitoes live on garbage and in the open drains [that ran before the houses] and cause infection: do cover the smallest scratch."

Rita Wenning had designed a camp emblem that was shown in the paper. "It is representing the British and The Netherlands flags. The cross formed between the flagstaffs symbolizes the cross we have to bear in common. The sparkling diamond in the intersection represents the noble effort of the internees of both nationalities to beautify their lives."

And beautify our lives we did in various ways. Some of the "English" instituted the ritual of morning "elevenses" (snack or beverage at eleven o'clock) and afternoon tea. Each *kongsi* member washed her hands, if there was water in the tap, combed her hair with the kongsi comb, and sat around a table of sorts. This was probably a crate or a plank on a suitcase, decorated with a flower if a bush near the barbed wire was in bloom.

The "tea" was a brew made from roasted rice. Invitees sipped genteelly from the half-coconut shells or chipped cups brought from home. Sometimes "cookies" were served—tiny rice patties baked on a tin. Spoons to stir the brew varied from a real silver spoon missed by the looters to a shoe horn; most resembled the little spoons used nowadays in Chinese restaurants. It was a hallowed rule that conversation on these occasions was not to be about the camp. Guests were often asked to tell a joke, recite a poem, or play a famous person in a game of charades.

At one of the tea charades, I arrived mimicking sleep by putting both hands together against an ear, cocking my head, closing my eyes. I had fastened a piece of paper with a letter "O" to my sun halter and stuck a long thin tail, its bushy end made from material scraps, to my shorts. I was Nap-O-Leon, and everyone guessed it.

In the camp I thought those make-believe teas silly. Now I realize that the structure and etiquette those meetings imposed helped to make an untenable living situation more tenable.

"Cultural" events took place. We already had our singing groups. Now lectures were presented out on Irenelaan at night. During the day it was too hot and the asphalt would stick to our bare feet—or to our behinds if we sat down. At night, a full or near-full moon would provide light to see by. The electric street lamps that had shined so brightly when we arrived had long remained dark because of the black-out.

Lecture subjects included butterfly collecting, astronomy, rubber harvesting, and whatever else anyone felt knowledgeable enough to talk about.

Lessons were popular among adults. Shelagh's mother taught beginning English to some of the Dutch, writing a primer with little pictures. Antoinette did Mensendieck exercises with any woman willing to get hot and sweaty doing knee bends and working her abdominal muscles.

I gave Dutch lessons to Australian nurses. The lessons were punctuated by roars of laughter as the girls attempted to pronounce the Dutch "g," and were discontinued when the group needed time to work on a mah-jongg set. With a pocket knife they chiseled wood out of the rafters and decorated the 144 domino-like tiles with signs drawn by a fellow-prisoner in her native Chinese.

For several months I took "Advanced English" from Ruth Russell-Roberts. She made sure my English sounded upper-class, and told me how to behave at hunts ("Call the red coats 'pink,' after a Mr. Pink, who designed them"), garden parties, horse races, cricket matches, the kind of events I had seen pictures of in the British society magazine *Tattler*. I felt I would fit right in if ever I attended one of those events when the war was over.

The concerts, teas, charades, lectures, and lessons all reflected the interests of the leisure-class women that most of us had been. These leisure activities kept us sane in the crushing boredom of internment, just as domestic skills—the womanly skills—kept us alive.

Ruth and I also met regularly at the end of the day to walk laps on Irenelaan. She was almost as tall as I, and in our identical camp costumes of shorts and halter top we looked alike, except for the straw boater hat Ruth wore on the back of her head even after the sun went down. The hat gave her a jaunty, rakish air and made her look too young to be the mother of the little girl she had sent from Singapore to England shortly after the Japanese invaded Malaya.

Ruth was very shy, and here, too, she and I were much alike. She talked little about her child, Lynette, but I gathered she was torn with worry. Was the girl safe in some English country village, far from the German air raids that must still be devastating London? And where was Ruth's husband, who had been serving in the British Army in Malaya? "If the Japanese would at least let us receive Red Cross messages," she said.

Shelagh was another of the English women I often walked with. We had both worked as secretaries in offices and had something to compare. She would tell me about what she called her "past sickness," her longing for lovely evenings when friends took her out.

"The boys looked so good in their mess kits. I felt nice in my evening dress and clean and lovely, and they appreciated my looking nice. And the little dinners we would have at home, and the tennis parties and all the fun—it is good to have had such good times so that we can remember them . . . But, oh, to have someone to make a fuss over me here."

☙ ☙ ☙

So we muddled along as a group, trying to make the best of it, to "count our blessings." Oh, there were chronic complainers, like the women Betty Jeffrey called "the hearts." They wailed about a heart condition that would prevent their participation in community chores. There were mothers who continuously bemoaned the absence of a local woman to take care of a child. In the Far East in those days it was not unusual for such a person to wake a child, bathe, dress, feed, tend him all day and put him to bed again. Now, suddenly, the mothers had to do all this. Some took their feelings of resentment out on the children. "Get out of the room, Jantje. I'm trying to roll up the beds so there'll be space for us to *sit*." "Don't shout, Muriel, I have a headache." "You horrible child, you got yourself dirty again, and I just washed your pants, and you know the water hasn't been turned on all day."

My sisters and I kept busy. Although we had entered the camp as a trio, and others spoke of us as "the three Colijn girls," we often saw each other only at meal times and during discussions about who was going to do what for our household. We now lived by rote. You do this today, I'll do it tomorrow.

As I befriended Shelagh and Ruth, Antoinette and Alette befriended members of the English singing groups and spent much time rehearsing for the latest show or songfest.

In addition, Antoinette was often trotting around doing something for someone else. Alette continued to mother little Wim and plod through *Les Misérables* with Sister Catharinia. I read through the library books.

We each sewed a dress from sarongs we had bought after the shipwreck. They were our "liberation dresses"—our "day-of-deliverance dresses," as some English called them—to wear when we would walk out of the camp. Mrs. van Zanen had shown us how to cut a pattern and sew pieces together by hand. Sewing, like cooking, had not yet been part of our education.

I also made a long-sleeved jacket out of gunny-sack material, open at the front and embroidered with cross stitching along the edges. The colors were red, white, and blue—the Dutch flag colors. I would have liked to add orange, the color of the banner flown along with the Dutch flag to honor the royal family of the House of Orange, but there was no orange thread in the camp. I was proud of my jacket.

Some Sundays I joined my sisters in English worship in Shelagh's garage, where her kongsi members had removed all bedrolls and pots and pans so they could have a service. It was often led by Miss Dryburgh. Her first name was Margaret, but I never called her that because of the age difference. She was in her early fifties.

When I first met Miss Dryburgh, she had struck me as a rather dull bird: eyes peering through thick round lenses, brownish hair in a tight bun at the back of her head, a short stocky figure wearing the sensible loose-fitting cotton dress and Mary Jane-type shoes she had worn on the *Mata-Hari* out of Singapore. But I soon discovered that Miss Dryburgh was not at all a dull woman.

I had already heard, that very first day in camp, part of her humorous "Palembang Camp Song" and watched a variety show she scripted. She also wrote little birthday poems and gallant tributes to those of us in camp. My sisters and I had been touched by her tribute to us:

And when at length they take their place
Within a world that needs brave youth,
May past experience add new grace,
Suffering give clearer view of truth,
May life hold many blessings yet
For Helen, Antoinette, Alette.

Apparently, she was good not only with poetry but with music as well. "She used to play the organ in our church in Singapore, in a great way," I was told. "She also taught fine piano to some of our youngsters."

In July 1942, Miss Dryburgh combined her poetic and musical talents and wrote the words and melody for "The Captives' Hymn."

"I was out flapping a fire when Miss Dryburgh thrust a piece of paper in my hands," Shelagh told me. "She said, 'We're singing this as an anthem. You have to practice it.' And it was very difficult to sing, really. The words meant a lot. It was difficult not to show emotion."

The hymn premiered on July 5, 1942, in the garage of house number

9. It was sung a cappella by Shelagh Brown, Dorothy MacLeod and Margaret Dryburgh, who sang the alto part.

Father, in captivity
We would lift our prayer to Thee,
Keep us ever in Thy love,
Grant that daily we may prove
Those who place their trust in Thee,
More than conquerors may be.

Give us patience to endure,
Keep our hearts serene and pure,
Grant us courage, charity,
Greater faith, humility,
Readiness to own Thy will,
Be we free or captive still.

For our country we would pray,
In this hour be Thou her stay,
Pride and selfishness forgive,
Teach her by Thy laws to live,
By Thy grace may all men see
That true greatness comes from Thee.

For our loved ones we would pray,
Be their guardian night and day,
From all dangers keep them free,
Banish all anxiety,
May they trust us to Thy care.
Know that Thou our pains doth share.

May the day of freedom dawn,
Peace and justice be reborn.
Grant that nations loving Thee
O'er the world may brothers be,
Cleansed by suffering, know rebirth,
See Thy kingdom come on earth.

I was as moved as Shelagh, but, like her, I didn't want to show it. At that time I viewed the hymn, particularly the fourth verse about the loved ones, in terms of the emotions it evoked in me—a tender, touching hymn. Now I see it as a statement by a generous, forgiving, and loving woman. She doesn't bother to say who the conquerors were—just as in the camp she never used the word Jap, and never such expressions as others threw out like "nasty little devils." She showed no bitterness or anger, only courage and hope that o'er the world nations may brothers be. Now I see Margaret Dryburgh's "Captives' Hymn" as an instrument of peace.

Chapter Eight

Meeting Beyond the Wire

Allowing us to perform skits and sing in church and concert choirs was a humane thing for the Japanese to do. After the war we learned that in some other internment camps singing or acting had been forbidden.

Another humane thing the Japanese did in the early part of our imprisonment—and humane for a reason other than they must have thought themselves—was allowing us to go for medical visits to the Charitas Hospital in Palembang. It was still staffed by Dutch Franciscan nuns, and Dutch Dr. Peter Tekelenburg was in attendance. His wife and two daughters were with us in the women's camp.

Once a week a wheezy old ambulance, its innards removed, called at our camp to pick up patients put on the Charitas list by our camp doctor, Jean McDowell.

Antoinette went for the infected shrapnel wound on her arm. Others went to have a tooth extracted, a boil lanced, or a prescription written for glasses. Several women had lost theirs in shipwrecks. Women also went to find out whether they were pregnant because their menstruation had stopped. This proved to be an unnecessary worry: very soon after we arrived in camp, menstruation stopped for all of us. Women who actually were pregnant when entering the camp went to Charitas to have their babies delivered there. The ambulance returned clinic patients the same day, and patients who were hospitalized, a week or two later.

The Charitas to which we were taken was not the brand-new hospital the nuns had moved into shortly before the war. The Japanese had requisitioned it for themselves and relegated the Charitas sisters to far less adequate, old facilities. Here the nuns, with medications and surgical equipment smuggled along, ably took care of sick from the local population, from the women's camp, and from the men internees' Palembang jail.

The three groups lived in separate quarters. Japanese orders were that they were not to communicate with, let alone visit, each other. I don't know how many of the hospitalized internees did make it to each other's wards to pass written or oral messages for someone in the opposite camp, or to actually meet with a spouse or friend. I do know that the hospital's Mother Alacoque was instrumental in maintaining a pipeline of secret correspondence between the two camps. She hid small folded notes under her voluminous skirt and carried them between the women's and men's wards. Patients returning to the women's camp or to the jail would then deliver the notes to the addressees. Women would sew the notes into the hems of shorts or in the straps of sunhalters or hide them on their bodies. Fortunately, our guards were not in the habit of frisking us.

Because of this Charitas pipeline, my sisters and I were finally able to hear from and write to Father. His notes were always short and noncommittal.

"What if he wants to tell us something important, news about the war, for example?" asked Antoinette one day. "He may have more information than we get here."

This led to our working out a code. It was a simple code and no doubt, from a detective's viewpoint, totally transparent. The key would be in the date at the top of the letter. The date would not be written in the Dutch manner, for example, "2 *augustus*, 1942" (with the day first), but in the American way, "August 2, 1942" (with the month first). The difference between month and day, in this hypothetical case six, would denote the keywords in the message. It took many weeks to notify Father of our code, in three different notes via the Charitas route.

The route came to a sad end when the Japanese apprehended Mother

Alacoque in the act of smuggling notes from the women's ward to the men's ward. She was interrogated and brutally treated by the *Kenpeitai*, the Japanese military police, and had to spend months in an isolation cell. The news of Mother Alacoque having been taken away (that she was tortured and condemned to solitary confinement, we heard only much later), and the end of the secret correspondence, hit the women's camp hard.

❧ ❧ ❧

Not long thereafter, when we had been about seven months in the camp, we were electrified by a piercing cry from a group of children, "Our meee-een!" "Our men are passing by!"

Most of us ran outside, climbed onto any high perches we could find, and shaded our eyes to look into the distance. And, yes, there was a group of men walking—they were white men wearing hats some women recognized as those of their husbands, and shirts that were familiar, too. Those who recognized men screamed "Piiieet," and "Joooohhhn," and waved frantically with their arms.

"Look," Antoinette whispered to me. She could hardly speak. "Look, Father is there too."

He was waving an orange flag. We waved back.

"I bet those nincompoops alongside them don't even know why he's waving an *orange* flag," said Alette.

Slowly, the procession of men continued, two abreast, flanked by their Japanese guards. Where were they going?

The ration truck driver informed us the next day. "They're building a new place for themselves, a barracks camp. The Japanese need the jail for the locals."

From then on, each day a group of our men passed our camp, several hundred feet away, going one way in the morning and back in the afternoon. English Mary always stood on the steps of her house on Irenelaan and waved a pink bathroom towel to her husband, with whom she had left Singapore. Dutch Marie posted herself at the intersection of our two camp streets and wore a brightly patterned shirt she had recently made from a batik cloth. Her husband, marching in the distance, wore a shirt of the same material.

109

There was much speculation in our camp about how these two identical shirts had come about. Marie wouldn't say. Much later we learned that her husband had sent her the batik clandestinely, via a woman patient in Charitas. Marie had cut the cloth in half, made two shirts, and sent one back to her man in jail along the same forbidden route.

Nel de Bert, the mother with four children with whom my sisters and I had shared a room the first night in the camp, lined up her daughter of seven and three younger brothers, two of them twins, on a small wall. She neatly combed each child's hair. "The men are too far away to see the children clearly, but I think it is important that the children look neat. This will give them an idea of good manners. It is hard to instill those here." The children waved dutifully when their mother told them to, but they looked solemn, and sometimes they cried. Where other children were waving to a father, theirs was not there.

Each day at the first cry of "Our meeeen," my sisters and I climbed a wall jutting out from house number 13, pulled ourselves up on a ledge of the red-tiled roof, catwalked over the pointed edge, and were all three sitting astride the nook by the time the marching men were level with the camp. We whooped what we as children had called the "Alpine cry," breathing a long "Hoooooo," tapping one hand in front of our mouths for a series of very short "hooo-hooo-hooos." We ended the staccato shout with a final high-low, "Yoo-hooo." After that we made the V for Victory sign with our arms, sometimes stretching our little towels between for better visibility.

The men went on their working parties in shifts. Father usually came on Mondays and Wednesdays. On days when we didn't expect Father, we climbed on the roof anyway. Someone else would report to him that we were all three on the roof, all three presumably well. So the Japanese let my sisters and me at least catch a glimpse of Father.

৵ৡ৽ ৵ৡ৽ ৵ৡ৽

One day the men were allowed to send us gifts. "Parcels from the meeeen!" shouted the children when the ration truck drove up. Next to the rotten *kangkung* lay bulging woven-grass bags, things wrapped in a piece of cloth or a neckerchief, a cardboard box, all with names written on them.

110

Antoinette, Alette, and I rushed up the hill and, yes, there also was a woven-grass bag with our names. Father sent us a shiny tin of KLIM and a five-pound tin of butter which looked as if they had just been purchased at a grocery store. Also in the parcel were *kacang hijau,* a coconut, and a bunch of bananas.

The bananas stunned us. Where in the world would Father have gotten those? Of course, bananas grew all around Palembang, but we never saw them in the camp. Because they were perishable, the vendor wouldn't bring them in. We decided the men must either be better negotiators than we were or still have a black market going with local people outside the jail. After the dreadful experience with the man tied to the pole, efforts of the women to obtain extra food from behind our barbed-wire fence had ceased.

The men, realizing that many women didn't have anyone in the jail and were therefore unlikely to receive a parcel, had also sent several woven-grass bags addressed "Women's Camp." Our Red Cross committee distributed these gifts among women whom they felt deserved them. This must have been a delicate task. Who deserved the men's gifts? All the women who had received nothing when the truck arrived? Only the women who received nothing but had no money of their own to procure extras from the vendor? Only women who received nothing, had no money, and were ill?

In December, when we had been more than eight months in the camp, more parcels from the men arrived. Again there was one from Father with our names on it. We rushed to our cubicle with it and began unpacking the bag.

"Oh look, soap," said Alette. As she picked up the square piece to display it with other gifts on the counter, the soap fell into two pieces.

"Look at this, Father must have cut it and stuck it together again to hide this," and she pulled a rolled-up note from a cavity in the soap.

"He never was any good with his hands," Antoinette said, tenderly.

"It's in our code!" she cried, looking over Alette's shoulder. "The date is written the American way." The note was dated December 17, 1942.

"The key is five," I said. "Quick, let's see what the message is."

Antoinette opened one of the notebooks she had bought and, as I read the letter aloud, she wrote down every fifth word.

Here is the letter in full: "In the evening at ten-thirty. The moon is rising behind the cells and the fence. How are you, your house is not too cramped? In eight days it will be Christmas. Strange to celebrate alone. I'll attend church services of course. Be sure you do, too. Comes 1943. Let us hope, if God wills it so, you will be home again. Can you imagine that? Cheerio."

And here is the message that emerged: "Ten-thirty behind fence house eight Christmas I'll be come if you can."

"Is he actually going to call on us?" asked Antoinette, incredulously.

"But how is he going to do it?" wondered Alette.

We decided that Father would have to sneak out on his working party at the men's new camp site and somehow cover the distance to our camp without being seen by either a Japanese guard or a *heiho* (a local man recruited as an auxiliary soldier). "It's going to be tricky," I said, and worried to myself. A Japanese soldier would probably shoot if he spotted Father or haul him off to the Kenpeitai. A heiho would be delighted to arrest a wandering Dutchman just to show the Japanese how efficient he was.

"Let's destroy the note, right now," Antoinette said, practically, and tore it up into tiny pieces, which she handed to me. "Here. It's your turn to cook dinner tonight. Use these to light the fire." She destroyed the notebook sheet too.

Christmas day arrived. At eight in the morning, at the children's cry, "Our meeen," Antoinette, Alette, and I climbed onto the roof of house number 13 with even more alacrity than usual, whooped our alpine cry, and made the V-sign with our arms. Father was in the men's party and waved to us with his orange cloth.

At 10:15 we left our cubicle, one after the other. Antoinette went first.

"Watch out for tattletales," I warned. There were women in the camp who might report us to the guard.

I went last. The camp was in a festive mood, and more women were out on Irenelaan than usual. An English woman stopped me and asked whether she would have a Dutch lesson from me that day. I said no, not on Christmas day. Another woman was eager to tell me all the details about two women in her house who were at daggers with each other over space in their room. I brushed her off, saying I was on my way to see friends in the Australian House. It happened to be next to house number 8. I reached the fence behind it without being seen.

I dropped on all fours and crawled under the wire. The Japanese must be confident we won't run away, I thought, or they would have erected a more formidable fence. I continued on all fours through the grass, which was in places almost half a meter tall. I was glad my camp costume was khaki.

I looked for Antoinette and Alette. It was so quiet. Where were they? Nothing stirred. Nothing breathed.

"Hey, you almost crashed into me," I heard Alette chuckle. She, too, was on all fours. Antoinette was crouched right behind her.

"Let's go a bit farther out," I whispered. "Father won't want to come too close to the women's camp."

We crawled another little distance and stopped in a clearing between bushes. There was no sign of father.

The dead silence continued. Nature seemed to hold its breath as I held mine. Not a leaf rustled. Not a branch swayed. My mouth was dry. My heart pounded. Had something happened to Father? Had the guard caught him as he sneaked away?

Then I saw him. He was standing motionless under a tree. He crouched, too, and came toward us in the clearing silently, slinking like a leopard through the grass. In one hand he held something tied in a red-checkered cloth. He put the bundle down and hugged us. Nobody said a word.

"Happy Christmas," Alette finally whispered, and the rest of us chorused, "Happy Christmas."

"How is your arm?" Father asked Antoinette, and she held it out to him so he could see the ten centimeter wide scar near her wrist.

"I'll buy you a bracelet, as I promised you in the jungle."

"Was it difficult to get here?" I wanted to know.

"It was easy to detach myself from the working party and crawl a good part of the way through the corn fields to your camp. The most difficult part was where I least expected it: I had just stood up and crossed a road behind the back of three Japanese soldiers when I met an old Chinese man. He asked what I was doing outside the campgrounds. I told him I wanted to see my three little girls and he let me pass."

"I brought you three a present," Father said, and handed Antoinette the bundle in the red-checkered cloth. "Don't open it now. It's a tin with chicken. I bought it on the black market. The chicken is already cooked."

"We have a present too," said Alette, and from her shorts' pocket she pulled a little folder she had covered with linen and embroidered with

Father's initials, A.C., in red and blue thread left over from my rice-sack jacket. "It has drawings inside made by one of the Dutch women. One shows the three of us sitting on the roof, waving at you."

Father looked at his watch, the same Swiss one he had had for years.

"The Japanese have offered me good money for this watch," he whispered, following my glance. "But so far I haven't needed the money. If I run out, I will let them have it. I have to go now. Otherwise, I won't be back in time for the end-of-the-morning roll call. If you see me in the working party when we pass the women's camp, you'll know I got back all right."

"If only Mother could know we are all together today," said Antoinette. "She must be so worried about us." As we are worried about her, I thought. What a ridiculous situation, a whole family broken and scattered without contact. I didn't know then that many thousands of families in the Dutch East Indies were in the same boat.

"Let's pray for Mother," Father said. Huddled together in the clearing behind the barbed-wire fence, we folded our hands, bowed our heads, and Father asked God to look after her. He gave each of us a quick kiss. "I have to go now. Keep smiling. It won't be long." And he was gone.

"You go back first," I said to Antoinette. "Alette and I will follow in a few minutes. Be careful with that chicken."

Antoinette went, clutching the red-checkered bundle to her chest and, in her agitation, walked boldly upright. Alette and I followed in the same manner.

"Our men . . ." cried the children. Antoinette, Alette, and I couldn't get up to the roof quickly enough. We had to see whether a shape waving an orange cloth was walking among the men. Father was there. We gave him the alpine cry with more gusto than ever.

As planned, the women sang, "Oh Come All Ye Faithful" and "Silent Night" for the men. High up on the roof I listened to the familiar carols.

Through a mist of tears, I saw the column of men stand still to listen.

Mac (the American journalist in my lifeboat) also was in the work party that day. Forty years later he would say, "Instead of screaming names, as the women always did, there was silence, dead silence. And suddenly we heard singing. Across the abyss between us came this beautiful 'Oh Come All Ye Faithful.' And then 'Silent Night.' We stood there with the guards around us. The guards—they were entranced too. It really was so moving, we wept. Even now I think how wonderful that was, to give us life."

➴   ➴   ➴

Soon after the beginning of 1943, the men moved to their new location and a gloom settled over our camp. No more did the men go by. Nor were they able to send gifts and clandestine messages.

The months passed. And one day, in the summer of 1943, the ration truck arrived with wood, after first delivering a load to our men. And among our load was a piece of wood on which was written in charcoal, "WE ARE GOING TO BANGKA."

This was appalling news. It had been such a good feeling, even for those without menfolk nearby, to know that they were still close. Now we would be separated by a long stretch of the Musi River and a stretch of open sea.

We had barely adjusted to this physical separation when more bad news shook the women's camp. We ourselves were to be moved. "Be ready in 24 hours and bring no more than you can carry," was the order.

We had then been 18 months in the houses camp.

The first group to leave was loaded onto trucks, still wondering what the destination would be. When the trucks returned for the second group, one of the Palembang drivers dropped the bombshell: "You are going to the barracks camp the men just left."

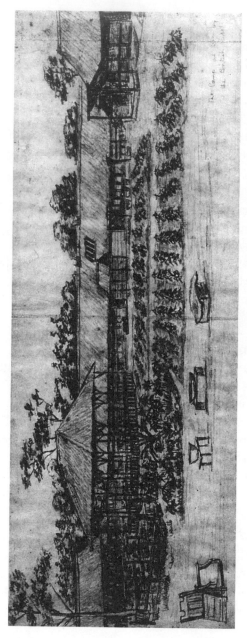

Margaret Dryburgh drew our second camp after the cassava-planting project mentioned later in the book. In the center is the pavilion we referred to with the Indonesian word *pendopo*.

Chapter Nine

First Barracks Camp: Community Living

Low we had all complained about conditions in the houses camp. The crowded rooms, the periodic turnoffs of the tap water, the monotonous, often filthy food. Compared with our new camp, the houses camp was a picnic.

This new camp was no larger than an American football field and consisted of a rectangle of dismal-looking barracks crudely built of bamboo-plaited *gedék* walls and palm-frond roofs. The rectangle enclosed a dusty or muddy compound. In the barracks were two bathrooms, a kitchen, a hospital (Charitas was closed), and accommodations for all of us in long rows on *balai-balai*'s, the kind of bamboo platforms my father and I had slept on in the first village after our lifeboat landing. When some 200 women and children from another now-liquidated camp and the white-robed sisters of Charitas (soon called the "White Sisters") were also squeezed into our camp, each person's space on the 1.80-meter deep balai-balai worked out to about 50 centimeters. So that was our *tempat* (a Malay word for space), our home to sleep, eat, and spend leisure time if it rained, a

117

home that measured 50 centimeters by 1.80 meters. Personal belongings were stored on each person's carefully measured 50 centimeters of shelf running along the barrack walls.

On this balai-balai we had no privacy. Neither did we have privacy in the communal bathroom. We had to stand naked in elbow-poking proximity to one another around a large, rectangular, empty water basin. In this camp, water came from wells. Balancing our containers of well water on the rim, we all soon became intimately familiar with everyone else's way of managing a bird bath with only one five-pound butter tin of rationed well water. Going to the bathroom at night with the idea of bathing in solitude was useless. There always would be women with the same idea.

Very unprivate, too, was the process of using the latrines—a row of little bamboo cubicles alongside the outer bathroom wall. Here we had to use an open drain behind swinging half-doors. Closed, the doors exposed our private parts when we squatted and our heads when we stood.

In the compound we could never be alone. Other women were always in the compound, walking ghostlike in the moonlight, their skin pallid, their steps languid and slow. We walked to look at the stars, or because we were going crazy with the itch. This was a new camp affliction: no rash or scabs formed, but the skin itched so badly that we wanted to scratch with our nails or a sharp object. This was unwise. Skin abrasions would develop into nasty, tropical sores.

Gone, too, in this camp were the small joys of the houses camp: the variety shows, the songfests, the books to read (the entire library had to be left behind), the lectures, the lessons among adults, the nuns' lessons to the children. All energies had to be channeled into a new kind of living: communal living. Now all of us had to "keep house" together, and had to volunteer for our share of *community* work.

Water squads hauled water in rusty buckets from the wells to the central kitchen for cooking rice and vegetables and boiling drinking water.

Vegetable squads, sitting on benches around a crude table near the kitchen, sawed through tough *kangkung* stalks with blunt knives and removed the most decayed leaves (time would come when we would eat those, too.)

Rice-picking squads cleaned the rice, spread it out on winnows, or poured it into a variety of pots. "The rice usually looked as if it was picked off the street, and was full of glass, stones, and dirt, not to mention hordes of fat maggots and weevils," wrote Miss Dryburgh, a frequent rice-picker, in her diary.

Dividing squads apportioned the drinking water boiled in the kitchen and the cooked food, of which there was less and less: so many portions in a large container, or a combination of small containers, for Barrack A; so many portions for Barrack B. Sometimes rations of salt, sugar, and red palm oil not used in kitchen cooking were apportioned to barracks, too. This way a woman could decide whether she wanted to add the palm oil (a thick oil that looked like tomato soup) to her morning rice porridge or add to the afternoon and evening rice for extra nourishment, or smear it on a tropical sore (some claimed it had healing powers), or use it with a wick in a coconut shell to make a nightlight for the children, to write a diary by or to read her Bible. Several Bibles had come into camp in women's personal luggage.

Deciding for ourselves what to do with the oil, sugar, or salt allowed us at least a scrap of individuality in our new communal world.

Bathroom squads cleaned the concrete floors of the smelly bathrooms Many women and children who had diarrhea often failed to reach the latrines in time. Also to be cleaned were the little planks over the latrine drain on which we had to put our feet. All this had to be done with little water and without soap or disinfectants. In the absence of brooms or brushes, the women who cleaned the bathrooms on their knees used shaggy coconut husks.

Latrine squads emptied the drains on each side of the camp. On the outside of the plaited bamboo walls, two women scooped the feces out of the latrine drain into containers with a tin or coconut shell nailed to a stick. A local man then removed the containers.

Antoinette and Alette had volunteered for a kitchen squad and stood atop of the stone fireplaces, often in smoke and stinging heat, to stir with long sticks the rice or vegetables in the drums. Or they squatted in front and tried to fan flames into the sputtering sparks fed by green firewood.

Little Wim, a toddler now, was tended by his mother. Alette said that that was O.K. by her. But she was disappointed that her French lessons with Sister Catharinia had come to an end. "Will I ever be able to catch up in school? I am already nearly two years behind."

119

Photos of our camps don't exist. These photos, taken right after the war, show conditions in Java camps similar to ours. (Top photo courtesy Museon, The Hague; bottom photo taken by J. Ulrich Kappler, a Swiss who was not interned and visited the women's camps on Java in search of Dutch friends.)

In charge of the kitchen were two women who worked every day—and most of the day unless they were ill—for the duration of captivity. These were British Norah Chambers and Dutch Saartje Tops. At four or five every morning, they rose to start the fires, wheedling the flames out of embers they kept alive from the previous evening. A match was a rarity in the camp.

At first, many of the jobs didn't have to be done daily. A sufficient number of women were still fit and willing enough to allow for a rotating work schedule.

As head of the wood squad, my community job was never daily. It depended on the delivery of wood for the kitchen. Whenever the children, still the camp messengers, cried, "Woood, wood has arrived," I gathered women on my list from both the "English" and the Dutch barracks. Pairs of us carried the wood from the gate to the kitchen. We laid the very long poles, the "trees," horizontally on our shoulders and carried them between us. We carried the chunks of wood, sometimes so heavy we could handle only one at a time, in a basket swinging from a bamboo pole that also rested on our shoulders.

It was important to have a partner of the same height, so a basket with wood wouldn't slide forward or backward on the pole toward the shorter of the two and land with a bang against her back or her bosom. The best way to walk was at a slight trot, keeping up a steady rhythm as, in precamp days, we had seen Chinese vendors do when they carried yokes hung at both ends with wares.

Being the head of a work team was a new experience for me, and I never did figure out how to convince someone on my list who was ten or fifteen years my senior—and whom I addressed as Mrs. or Miss—to get off the platform and pitch in when she said, "Sorry, not today, I think I'm going to be sick," or, pointing to a neighbor, "Ask her. She hasn't done a spot of work for weeks."

Since we were equally tall, I often carried wood with Ruth, my "upper-class-English teacher" of the houses camp. She still wore her boater hat, but the brim was raveled at the edges now. She had arrived in the camp with a beautiful slender figure, but was now so thin that her bones stuck out. Already, in the houses camp, we had exhausted discussions on such high-society events as following the hounds or playing cricket. Now we played the game of daydreaming.

The hard work of the kitchen crews was the same in all women's camps. Note fireplace with the tree in it. (Photo by J. Ulrich Kappler taken in Camp 10, Banjoe Biroe)

One morning I noticed that the bamboo pole between us made the same creaking noise as my saddle made when I rode horseback with my family in Holland. The dismal barracks, the dry-season dust swirling up in the compound, were gone. I was cantering along a Dutch beach. I pressed my legs against the horse's soft, warm flank. The wind blew across my face. The air had a salty tang. I saw the sand dunes that protect Holland's coast, and the dark green sea that washes Holland's shores. White caps curled, rolled over, disappeared, and made an ever-changing pattern on the water.

"What are you thinking about?" Ruth asked me.

I told her about my daydream, and then she told me one of hers. Soon it became a habit for the two of us to "go daydreaming," sharing lovely memories of the past as we hauled wood to the prison camp kitchen.

We trotted slowly. Though young, we were no longer strong. The heat was humid and oppressive, and even seemed to affect the guard. At least he didn't get off his chair in the guardhouse to cry "*lekas, lekas*," quickly.

Ruth told me of her stay in India before she married. Her fiancé was stationed somewhere as an officer of the British Army. With the snowcapped Himalayas in the background, the two would go boating on the lakes of Srinagar in a *shikara*. "That's a kind of floating sofa," Ruth said, "paddled by three boatmen: one would play the ukulele and the other two sang popular Kashmir songs."

I had no such romantic outings to relate but shared with Ruth happy memories of days with my sisters and parents skating in Holland, climbing mountains, or skiing in the Alps. Ruth also loved sports and wide open spaces.

Ruth and I preferred our game of daydreaming to the more popular camp game of collecting recipes. In tiny letters on precious scraps of paper, women would copy recipes from each other for fancy sauces and complicated desserts. Aloud, they'd then eat festive phantom dinners with mouthwatering foods. As they ate a minute portion of rice, they pretended it was roast beef with Yorkshire pudding or Dutch steak with gravy. They said it made them feel the hunger less.

As head of the wood squad, I had to go to the guardhouse to deal with the guard. Until then, I had had to see a guard only during daily roll call. I could usually keep him out of my sight for the rest of the day. Particularly in this new camp, it was easy to avoid him, for he no longer came stomping through to turn everything upside down in a blitzlike search for "weapons"

Childhood activities, from holding baby tigers in the Amsterdam zoo to boating in Austria, were subjects of daydreaming when I carried wood with Ruth.

such as razor blades and diaries he never found. But now I had to walk up to the guard, bow deeply, and tell him there was no wood left in the kitchen, a phrase I learned to say in Japanese: "*Maki wa arimasen,*" there is no wood. And when the wood was delivered, I had to say, "*arigato,*" thank you.

Sometimes he was quite human and, calling me *Si Panjang,* Tall One, he said in Malay, "Si Panjang, there is no wood, I am sorry." My height would make another guard furious. He would plant himself on the porch of the guardhouse and make me stand at the bottom step, so I wouldn't tower over him, and he would hurl Japanese sounds at me that I didn't understand. In spite of the guards' often bad feelings, I managed to get in and out of the camps without once being slapped.

The community chores became subjects of heated camp discussions. After a few months, owing to the continuing decrease in rations and the spread of malaria and dysentery, camp health had plummeted. When "the hearts" and others who didn't seem worse off than anyone else, refused to report to work, other women had to substitute. After awhile, the same women were doing all the work.

"This camp is a beehive," said Ruth to me. "We have our workers and our drones."

"How do we get the drones to work?"

We didn't have an answer, and no one else did, either. The camp representatives had no way of enforcing their authority. They had been chosen by the camp to represent us with the guards, and few considered their word law. And what if we had granted them authority? What could they have done to enforce rules? Levy a fine? Make someone do a nasty job? "You empty the latrines five days in a row," in a variation of a school teacher's punishment? Someone once suggested to Mother Laurentia that the shirkers be denied food, on the principle that, if you are unwilling to help prepare it, you have no right to eat it. But Mother Laurentia quickly brushed the idea aside. "It would be a sin to deprive anyone of food in our miserable conditions."

One way to attract workers was perks, the benefits that came with certain jobs. Emptying the latrines was a risky job. Coming in contact with feces could easily lead to dysentery, transmitted by flies. So the perk of this job was a tin of warm water from the kitchen for washing up afterward Cooking was arduous, too, and the cooks and their helpers were sooty and sweaty when they went off duty. They also were entitled to warm water from the kitchen. An extra water ration was always welcome, especially in times of drought. A ration of *warm* water was the apex of camp luxury.

The small boys who chopped the kindling for the kitchen fires were allowed to scrape the bottom of the rice drum. As soon as the kitchen staff put the drum outside, the boys dove in head first, little behinds sticking out, bandaged legs thrashing in the air. I could hear the muffled sounds as they bumped into each other and pushed each other at the bottom of the drum. Then they'd come up with a crust of rice, sometimes golden brown, sometimes burned black, scraped off the bottom with a piece of wood. This crust, even black, was savored as a delicious cookie. The boys would pool the scrapings and, with much concentrating, measuring, and checking, divide them up.

Whether a crust formed at the bottom of the drum, and how much did, depended on the amount of water added to the rice and the temperature of the fire. Sometimes a noncook accused a cook of letting a crust form on purpose. "What can you expect? She has a son in the kindling squad." But more crust meant less rice for the rest of us.

Were the given perks fair? This subject, too, was hashed out on both sides of the camp.

Why give warm water to cooks and not to vegetable cutters? Cutting vegetables wasn't arduous, true, nor was it a risk to health. But the cutter had to sit for hours among repulsively smelly greens. And hacking those leathery kangkung stalks was hard on the hands.

Should perks be given at all? Weren't we all in this together? Shouldn't everyone just help for the common good, without rewards? Years later in Menlo Park, P.T.A. mothers and I had a similar discussion: should the children be paid for making their beds or cleaning their rooms? Or should these chores be considered part of maintaining a home together?

Perks remained part of the camp picture until freedom came. My sisters enjoyed theirs, and I enjoyed mine. Members of the wood squad, another arduous job, received slivers of wood as a reward. The slivers were treasured for kindling to light a private fire. One of the head cooks doled them out in the kitchen.

Of all the hardships in this barracks camp, the absence of our men hurt most keenly. Not only did they not pass the women's camp anymore allowing us to wave and yell, they were completely gone from the scene, sent to an island called Bangka, and we never received an inkling of news from or about them.

Then, one day, the children ran through the camp shrieking, "There's mail, mail from the men on Bangka!"

A guard gave a cloth bag to one of the two camp representatives, who had run to the gate at the children's cry. The two took the bag to the *pendopo*, a little open hut with a peaked palm-frond roof in the center of the compound. Women thronged around the bag, impatient when the distribution did not proceed immediately. Unperturbed, the camp representatives asked that a table and bench be brought so they could sit down to their work.

Mother Laurentia opened the bag and began reading off names. None of the missives were in envelopes. Maybe those were not allowed. All the notes were folded several times. Ours was on a sheet of lined paper folded down to the size of a playing card.

"Helen, Antoinette, and Alette Colijn" was penciled on the outside in Father's strong, clear handwriting.

We read it on our space on the balai-balai.

23 November, 1943. Physically further separated, spiritually more united than ever. Instead of alamanda, my immediate view has now become a huge durian tree with a bright beyond. Except for itch troubles, I am all right. And you? This letter must be short. Therefore, heaps of kisses and love."

"Where do you think that alamanda grew?" Antoinette asked. She was familiar with the alamanda bush, with its yellow, chalice-shaped flowers; one grew in our parents' garden on Java. "If we knew, we would be able to tell which barrack he lived in.

"The men must have chopped it down when they knew they were going to leave here, to use the wood for a fire, or to eat the leaves. Who knows?" said Alette.

Now the men had written to their wives and children. Men who had no next-of-kin in the camp had written to women they barely knew or had merely heard about from other men. But together with the notes in the bag came a piece of paper with the names of men who died on Bangka who had wives in our camp. Dr. Mac and Mother Laurentia had to tell the widows. These grieving women had no place to hide, no place to be alone to absorb their awful news. One of them was in my barrack, and at night I heard her cry. But the next morning she said to me, "At least I don't have children," and from then on she acted as she had before she learned of her loss. And those of us who received letters thought, what kind of terrible place is that Bangka? Those men who died were in the prime of their lives. What is going to happen to the other men? What is going to happen to us?

Our spirits were flagging as 1943 drew to an end. It became obvious that we would be spending a second Christmas in captivity. Though it was harder and harder to believe that the war would be over in six months, most of us persisted in saying it would.

Our group of once healthy, husky women was losing more and more weight, getting increasingly sick, finding it ever harder to keep up spirits.

How we missed the cooking *kongsis* of the houses camp. There, at least, we had been able to decide when and how to cook our rations. We had been able to retain at least some of our individuality. Now we had to respond to the calls of bells, to pick up our meals, to do this or do that, as the guards and the group dictated. "If this goes on for long, we'll be reduced to a grey mass of regimented, automated prisoners," Antoinette said once.

Then Margaret Dryburgh and Norah Chambers saw a way to improve our camp morale. They announced another concert. A new choir would sing, recruited from both the "English" and the Dutch sides of the camp. Norah would conduct. The date was set for December 27, 1943.

Chapter Ten

Vocal Orchestra Concerts

The day of the concert had arrived.

The camp still didn't know what the program would be. The new choir had been practicing in a shed off the kitchen in the greatest secrecy. But those of us not involved with the program sensed that it was going to be something special. In my barrack, several women were "dressing up" for the event.

I, too, had been caught by the wave of excitement and was wearing the liberation dress I had not touched since I made it a year before in the houses camp. It had been stored in my woven-grass bag to wear on the day the Allies would come and rescue us. Now the dress was wrinkled, and mildewed, and smelled musty, but . . . it was a dress.

Alette and Antoinette were not wearing their dresses. "Not everyone in the choir has one," Antoinette explained, "so we'll all wear our regular camp togs."

"Enjoy our surprise," said Alette, and left with Antoinette to join the choir in the practice shed.

They haven't lost their allure, I thought. Antoinette, her hair pencil-straight now that her pre-war permanent had grown out and in her shorts and halter, made me think of a young page in a medieval painting, ready to run into battle with his lord. Alette looked graceful, as she did in my favorite photo of her when she was three, taken in our garden in The Hague. In the photo, Alette wore a brief, green silk tunic with pink silk roses sewn on here and there. She stood with one bent knee raised, bare toes pointing down, and held a little wooden flute she pretended to play. Her silky blond hair reached to her shoulders and was crowned with a wreath of the same pink roses as on the dress. She had danced in this costume on the stage of the Royal Theatre in The Hague in a benefit performance of a rhythmic dancing school we three girls attended once a week.

I picked up my half coconut shell from our storage shelf, slid off our *tempat* onto the aisle between the *balai-balai's*, and walked slowly toward the barrack exit. The day before, a torrential rain again cascaded through gaps in the palm-frond roof and left several puddles in the aisle. Mud now squished between my toes, and I worried that mud would spatter my dress.

I stopped to talk to one of the Dutch school teachers—I think she came from a small place inland—who was kneeling on her bed space and patting her sleeping pad. It was no thicker now than its two rice-sack covers put together, the dried grass inside had long ago flattened out.

"Beastly humidity. This thing got rained on yesterday, and it still isn't dry. I say, Helen, you look chic."

"Chic, I don't know about that . . . Anyway, more festive than my faded daily costume. It's my liberation dress. Are you going to wear something special?"

"I wish I had something. Like you, I saved a dress for when we get out, but last week someone sold it for me on the black market. A duck egg, some sugar, and chilis *now* will do me more good than a dress later on."

Would the time come when I would have to sell my dress?

A few tempats away a woman, whom my sisters and I called Mrs. Sargeant Major, was sitting on her mattress pad. I was sure she would have something unpleasant to say, and she did.

"All dolled up. You must be going to that concert. It's absurd to waste precious energy singing. The singers should be using their energy for just staying alive!"

130

"But the singers say they generate energy by singing."

"Could be. But we all know the Japanese don't want us to gather in crowds. To have a whole mass of us in the compound, listening to I don't care what, is inviting disaster. The guard will lose his temper and we'll all have to stand in the sun again. *I* am *not* going."

"A pity." She's as impossible as ever, I thought, and still in good shape. Too bad some who would have loved to go to a concert are not in the shape she is. Here and there, all through the long barrack, women and children were lying on their tempats with malaria or dysentery.

Not far from Mrs. Sargeant Major, one of the mothers called to her seven-year-old, who was banging with a piece of wood on the balai-balai. "Annie, let's forget about killing cockroaches now. I want to make your hair look pretty." She took a piece of red ribbon from a Quaker Oats tin (which evidently was her treasure box) and tied a bow in the girl's blond curls. The mother then called her ten-year-old son, who was "foot skating" on the mud in the aisle. "Enough of that, Jan, you are making the aisle more slippery yet. If you come here, I'll fix your hair too."

While the boy stood at the edge of the platform, his mother dipped her fingers into a battered enamel cup filled with water she must have hauled from the well or maybe collected in yesterday's downpour. She wetted the boy's hair and combed it with a tiny pocket comb. Then she held up what once must have been her purse mirror for the two children to view themselves. The girl looked puzzled. She probably couldn't remember the last time she had worn a ribbon in her hair. I saw the boy's eyes light up. He said, "Wow," sucked in his breath, and puffed out his little naked chest. This made his ribs stick out even more.

"Here, Jan, scrape the mud off your feet and try not to collect mud again before we go to the concert." The mother handed him a sliver of wood. "You two may sit in front of the audience with the other children. But you *have* to sit still, even if the music is 'grown-up' music."

She turned to me. "I'm so glad there is some entertainment again. In the houses camp there was always something going on, also for the children. Poor things, nothing to do for them here. They miss school . . . But what is the program going to be? Everyone is so mysterious about it. With your sisters in the choir, surely you know?"

"I wish I did. The girls only told me that there are 30 singers, from both sides of the camp. The language barrier doesn't seem to matter."

"Don't forget to bring cups for the refreshments," I reminded the mother, and picked my way further down the dark barrack to the exit. When my eyes had adjusted to the outside glare of the sun, I saw, to my relief, that the compound had dried out already.

It looked just as it did when I crossed it earlier that day: the same rectangle of barracks, the outer perimeter of our camp, the same sad-looking laundry festooning the fronts of the sleeping barracks, the same giant mushroom, our *pendopo* hut, in the center. But the compound was now full of women and children with a festive air. It had been a good idea going from barrack to barrack to announce the concert.

When Antoinette had asked me to do that, I had protested, "Everyone knows already there will be a concert."

"But if you take the trouble to *announce* it, it will add importance. Get yourself a tin and a stick and cry out the news, like an old-fashioned town crier."

Antoinette was so eager and looked so strangely happy that I had humored her. For a drum I had used the five-pound butter tin we used for drawing water from the well, and I had made the rounds, self-consciously beating the tin with a borrowed wooden spoon and making my announcement.

In the compound little boys and girls now strutted about, groomed with a special combing of the hair or wearing a shirt. English women wore their long-saved "day of deliverance" dresses, bright and cheerful touches of color in the crowd. One matron, never one to take care of herself, now sported with a pleased air a frowsy, purple housecoat.

"Mrs. Rich," a rubber planter's wife from Malaya, wore one of the designer dresses she had brought with her in expensive suitcases and had consistently refused to share or sell. "They're the only possessions I have left."

The Australian nurses must have shared a lipstick. They all wore the same shade, a flaming red that made their faces look even more sallow than their usual prison camp pallor.

A British Eurasian, a thin, still handsome woman with coal-black hair and big brown eyes, wore a twig with greenery behind her ear. She must have snitched it from a bush behind the guardhouse. Nothing grew in the camp.

Annie, Jan, and their mother came up from behind me and walked to the pendopo. Passing me, Annie pointed to the ribbon in her hair with a little giggle. I saw the three fold themselves onto the dirt floor of the pendopo, the children in the front row with other children, the mother a few rows behind.

Someone had scratched letters on one side of the dirt floor that two of the Sisters of Carolus Borromeus, acting as ushers, were keeping clear. O R C H E S T R A, I read. Was someone trying to be funny? There wasn't a single musical instrument in this camp. Surely we weren't going to have a concert with cymbals made from empty tins or flutes from pieces of firewood? A tall, wooden crate, presumably to be used as a lectern, stood forlornly in the empty space.

The program was scheduled for 4:30, after we were served an early dinner, and I knew that Norah, the conductor, would start on time in order to be done before darkness fell. Only a few timepieces were working in the camp, and Norah probably had asked the one Australian Army nurse who still had a watch to warn her of the time.

The weather was holding.

The pendopo was far too small to seat everyone. Already people were sitting on the pendopo railings and standing in rows outside. I was also standing. Just as well. It would be painful to sit with my "Palembang bottom." I had just discovered a new boil. And I might ruin my liberation dress sitting on the ground. Being tall, I could stand in the back row and still see what was going on.

At 4:30 sharp, 30 women filed behind Norah Chambers from behind the central kitchen toward the pendopo. Each carried pieces of paper in one hand and a little stool in the other. I saw no instruments.

They were wearing their camp togs all right, faded shorts and halter tops or much-mended faded, cotton dresses, in some instances shortened at the hem to provide material for needed patches.

They wore their hair straight down, held out of the face with a bobbypin, or cut very short like a boy's, on account of head lice.

Most of the singers were barefoot and had grubby bandages around their legs or feet to cover tropical sores. A few wore mud-caked *terompah*'s, wooden sandals with cloth or rubber straps over the toes, the kind we used to wear in our spacious, Dutch-East-Indies bathrooms, as we dipped clean,

Norah Chambers as student at the
Royal Academy of Music in London.
The red sash meant she played in the
orchestra.

cool, refreshing water out of a big basin and splashed it over ourselves.
"You must protect your feet from infections you might pick up if you stand
barefoot on the bathroom floor," I heard Mother say to us girls. My dear
mother, where was she now?

The singers sat down on their stools, except for Norah Chambers and
Margaret Dryburgh, who came in with the altos. Norah was dressed in a
shirt and a pair of new-looking beige slacks that one of the Dutch women
had given her upon arrival in the houses camp. Norah was another shipwreck survivor. Miss Dryburgh wore the dress she had entered the houses
camp with, but the flowers had disappeared in the wash and sunshine, and
the fabric hung loosely around her pared-down shape. She still had the
same hairdo, long hair tied in a bun at the back of her head. Her Mary
Jane-type shoes were held together by pieces of string. After a conspirato-
rial wink to Norah, she placed her music scores on her stool and faced the
audience with a piece of paper in her hand, from which she read:

"This evening we are asking you to listen to something quite new, we are sure: a choir of women's voices trying to reproduce some of the well-known music usually given by an orchestra or a pianist. The idea of making ourselves into a vocal orchestra came to us when songs were difficult to remember, and we longed to hear again some of the wonderful melodies and harmonies that uplifted our souls in days gone by. So we make our humble attempt to let you hear some of the masterpieces of the musical world as well as we can remember them: Dvořák's "Largo" from the New World Symphony, with its haunting negro melody; one of Brahms' sprightly waltzes; Mendelssohn's Song without Words; the string quartet music of Tchaikovsky's Andante Cantabile, where you may pick out the cello solo if you listen; and Chopin's Raindrop Prelude, with its persistent dropping accompaniment (so like what we hear every day and night!). Everyone will recognize the "Londonderry Air," and Beethoven's dainty minuet; and we include the delicate music of the "Faery Song" from Rutland Boughton's The Immortal Hour. And, most ambitious of all, Debussy's "Rêverie," which we know will soothe away all worries and vexations. The program will close with a selection of Christmas music and "Auld Lang Syne."

"We do not profess to reproduce the effects or quality of stringed or reed instruments. But as the lovely melodies and harmonies of the Great Masters greet your ears, you may imagine you hear them. The choir will remain sitting, as does an orchestra, to conserve their energies. Mrs. MacLeod is contributing two solos to the program, "The Lord Is my Light" and "Here in the Quiet Hills," thus enabling the performers to rest for a short while. And to give them a further chance of recuperating, there will be an interval of 20 minutes when refreshments will be provided for all, thanks to the generosity of the Dutch ladies. The Australian sisters are kindly serving the coffee.

"So close your eyes, and try to imagine you are in a concert hall hearing Toscanini or Sir Thomas Beecham conduct his world-famous orchestra."

So *that* was the surprise, orchestral and piano music in a place without musical instruments, not even a pitch pipe. At concerts in the houses camp Miss Dryburgh had always given the pitch. She did so now, after taking her place again in the alto section.

Norah Chambers, her back now turned to us, raised her hands. The choir started to sing, "leh, leh, leh," in four-part harmony. Very softly, as through a haze, the first measures of Dvořák's "Largo" came floating through the pendopo. The music slowly swelled. A solo joined in. It was the deep voice of Miss Dryburgh. The music soared into its first rich and full crescendo. I felt a shiver go down my back. I thought I had never heard anything so beautiful before. The music didn't sound like a women's chorus singing songs. It didn't sound precisely like an orchestra either, although it was close. I could imagine I heard violins and an English horn. The music sounded ethereal, totally unreal in our sordid surroundings.

"Huu, huu," I heard behind me. It was the ugly, raw voice of an angry guard. No doubt he had his bayonet ready. No one in the back row looked behind her, and neither did I. Norah must have heard the guard, too. Would she stop conducting? Norah went on waving her hands.

"Huu, huu," I heard again. The guard was now close behind me. He must have reached almost the back row. I stepped aside, as did others, to let him pass. Yes, he did have the bayonet on his rifle. And he was clearly furious. The line of women closed up behind him. He was shorter than most of us and disappeared from view. I could just see the top of his hated cap, with its stupid ear flaps, and the tip of his bayonet gleaming in the setting sun. He reached the railing of the pendopo. Surely he would explode, face to face with the singing choir. I couldn't see the tip of his bayonet anymore. Had he put the rifle down? And I did not hear anymore "Huu, Huu's." Could he be listening to the music? As the Largo moved toward a great, glorious crescendo, the guard remained as still as we. He remained still during the rest of the program.

I missed parts of the concert, overtaken as I was with intense memories.

The "Raindrop Prelude" took me back to a youth concert in The Hague, where I had gone with friends from my *gymnasium* class. I was 16 then and had met Henk, a year my senior. I remembered how he took me on my first date, two years later, when I was living with my grandparents while I finished high school. Henk, being one year ahead, was a first-year university student, and had picked me up in his father's car. We went to a movie about Ferdinand de Lesseps, who built the Suez Canal. Tyrone Power played de Lesseps.

I had never seen anything but Shirley Temple movies, and was excited at going to an adult film. But my grandmother frowned upon the outing. She didn't believe in movies, even Shirley Temple had seemed suspect to

First page of the handwritten score of the Largo. (Photo courtesy Department of Special Collections and the University Archives, Stanford University Libraries, Palo Alto, California)

her, but I had convinced her that this was an educational movie. Soon, on my shipboard voyage to my parents in the Indies, I would be passing through the Suez Canal, and I would know something about its construction. Grudgingly, Grandmother had given her permission. But I had to be home at eleven. Since the movie wasn't over until 11:30 Henk and I didn't see the end.

We had been asked to hold applause until the intermission. When the applause began, it was hesitant at first. The guard, after all, was still in our midst. But he, too, seemed to be savoring memories behind his stony face, and the applause slowly took on volume until it surged into a loud outpouring of enthusiasm, with cries of "Jolly good!" (from the "English") and "*Bravo*" (from the Dutch).

The members of the "vocal orchestra" looked at us with big smiles. Will they get up and bow, I wondered. No, why should they. The guard might think they are bowing to him, to the Emperor of Japan.

The singers returned to the kitchen area, and the audience began milling about. The Australians poured their promised "coffee" from the same odd assortment of sooty tins and pouring cans that we had been accustomed to seeing at entertainment in the houses camp. The coffee was served "black," but, oh bliss, it was *hot*. Any drink served through the community kitchen was cold by the time it was divided per barrack and then subdivided and poured into each person's cup.

In the meantime, Dutch women went around with little boards and a few real plates on which rested the by now familiar dime-sized cookies made of rice flour and water, this time with sugar. The cookies had a distinctly *sweet* taste.

I saw one of the servers offer a cookie to the guard, who looked oddly alone in a sea of captive women. He accepted and said "*Arigato*." I wondered, briefly, whether he had ever heard Western music. Was it the newness of our music that had enchanted him into quiet? Or had he heard Western music in Japan? Had it brought back memories to him as it had to me?

Now I think the guard may have been as lonely as we were, caught up in the idiocies of war. We were suffering from being cut off from our relatives, but perhaps he hadn't heard from his family in Japan either.

As the concert continued, I took a good look at who sang in Margaret Dryburgh's "vocal orchestra."

From the "English" side of the camp were Betty Jeffrey, Mickey Syers, and Flo Trotter, three of the Australian nurses who had taken my Dutch lessons in the houses camp when most of us were still full of energy and enterprise. I saw Shelagh, who in the early months of captivity had first sung the "Captives' Hymn" in a trio during an English church service, Audrey Owen, and Norah's sister Ena Murray, who had worked so hard in the houses camp stage-managing shows. I was glad to see her in this choir, she had a lovely soprano voice.

From the Dutch side of the camp I saw two other sisters of Carolus Borromeus, one of them Sister Catharinia. Only yesterday she had perched on top of my barrack in the downpour trying to repair the roof, her blue dress hoisted up so that her cotton bloomers showed. A black triangle was now tied jauntily over the thick blond hair that hung in a braid down her back. This was a very different Catharinia from the one who entered the camp with a demure, face-hugging wimple and a long, white habit.

Sigrid Stronk, one of the Dutch mothers, sang in the vocal orchestra, too. She had come from a palm oil plantation with a nine-month-old baby and a six-year-old boy. Mrs. de Bert was there, her four children sitting quietly with the other children in the front row. And there was Nel, who had been invited by the Japanese to live outside because she was part Asian but decided to stay with us.

The "Rêverie" took me back to Tarakan, where a visiting pianist had once played the "Rêverie" in the club. Father had looked constrained because he had to wear his white tuxedo jacket and formal shirt with black tie, but Antoinette and I were happy in long dresses. How grown up I had felt then, with the little black velvet band around my neck. How lovely and poised Mother had looked that evening. Again I wondered, with a deep gnawing anguish, where is she now?

The Christmas medley began with the "Pastorale" of Handel's *Messiah* and moved into an arrangement of Christmas carols, sung without words. The medley took me back to a time when Antoinette and I were both in high school in Holland and we spent Christmas vacation in England so we could improve our English.

We stayed with a family friend in a Norfolk village and took long walks in blustery winds on the moors and beaches with the three sons of a neighboring vicar. On Christmas Eve they had come caroling to the house

Sigrid Stronck, shown in 1945 with her two children, sang in the vocal orchestra.

where we were staying. Back in Holland, I received a tender letter from the eldest son, the first letter like that I ever received from a boy. Chris and I wrote letters, with big gaps in between, until he entered the British Army and was sent to fight in North Africa. He was a soft-spoken redhead with freckles and dimples. After the war I learned that he was killed near El Alamein.

"Now let's all sing 'Auld Lang Syne,'" Norah said, after the vocal orchestra sang its wordless version. "It's almost New Year's Eve."

It wasn't a song the Dutch often sing and I didn't know the words, but the British and Australians surely did, and sang with gusto.

Then the concert was over. We always called it "the Christmas concert," although the date was December 27.

The Japanese guard clomped back to the guardhouse.

"Good riddance to him," one woman said.

With the guard gone we were more relaxed, and we carried on after-the-concert conversations that belonged to other times.

"I would be happy if I had only heard the Largo."

"Don't you think they sang it too slowly?"

"Of course not, it *has* to be sung slowly."

"Which piece did you like best?"

"No preference. The music was all so marvelous."

"I would choose the Andante. It was so serene."

"When I heard the 'Raindrop' . . . somewhere in London, Covent Garden, I think it was. Quite an evening then, everyone dressed to a T, and to hear the same music now here . . ."

"I haven't felt so good since I entered the camp."

Yes, I thought, that music made a difference. I had been worried at the idea of having to stand so long, but I didn't feel tired at all.

With others I ambled back to my barrack. I crawled on the balai-balai, dimly lit by one of the few anemic light bulbs hanging above the aisle. Night had fallen suddenly, as it does in the tropics.

I packed my dress away and put my shorts and sun halter back on. Like most other women in the camp I now slept in my clothes. This permitted quick dashes to the latrine at night without anxiety about running into a rare patrolling guard.

Antoinette and Alette also returned and put their choir seats on the shelf. Pieces of wooden furniture left outside might be taken by someone in need of fuel.

We three strung up our mosquito nets. Around us other women who had gone to the concert were doing the same. Those who hadn't gone were already under theirs. "Come and tell me more about the music," I said to my sisters.

Antoinette and Alette slid under my net. Compressing ourselves as small as possible, arms around bent knees, heads lowered, we huddled together and whispered.

"I'm sorry you couldn't sing with us," said Antoinette. "We had such a good time at the rehearsals."

"Oh, but I had a good time listening to you," I said. When I wasn't transported elsewhere by memories, I thought.

I noticed Alette had brought a copybook. "Did you bring your vocal orchestra scores?"

Alette opened the copybook and held it up to me. "Here is what the Largo looks like."

"How can you read those tiny notes?

"We have to write this small, of course, because paper is so scarce. Shelagh used backs of tobacco plantation reports she found in the garage of house number 9. Sister Catharinia donated exercise books out of the little stash the nuns brought from the Lahat school. Antoinette and I are lucky to still have copybooks left from the supply we found in the houses camp. With 30 singers and 12 vocal orchestra pieces we needed a lot of paper."

Antoinette pointed with pride to the staves of Largo. "Drawn by hand, without ruler."

141

"How did you manage to get the lines so straight and an equal distance apart?"

"Eye-balling."

Antoinette had become one of the vocal orchestra's scribes. She copied scores from Norah's for herself and then for other singers. "Several of us don't know how to write music."

"And the pencils to write the music with, where did you get those?"

"Guess who produced four new pencils for the choir?" asked Antoinette, "and indelible pencils, at that."

"No idea."

"'Mrs. Rich.'"

"She of the matched suitcases?"

"Yes, hers truly."

"How much did she sell the pencils for?"

"She gave them to us."

"Gave them? I don't think she has given anything away in all the time we've been in camp."

"Quiet! Stop that whispering!" shouted someone further down the balai-balai.

"Well, we'd better end this for now," I suggested.

The girls went back to their own nets. Both looked tired but happy and Antoinette said, "It has been a truly wonderful day."

♫   ♫   ♫

In the early days of the houses camp Margaret Dryburgh wrote a long poem called "In foreign land we lived interned," that contained the lines:

"A sudden thought the mind did cheer
Much music that Thou once did hear
Is stored in memory
It lives forever. Bring it forth
Use our own instrument of work
Sing. Thou wilt happier be."

While in the camp, Rita Wenning made this artistic interpretation of the Largo in tones of brown and green as a gift for Norah Chambers. She relied heavily on white shoe polish that made it into the camp.

She then had probed her memory, and urged others to probe theirs, as she wrote in her poem, for "old songs of school days, college glees, ditties of home, comedies, anthems of nobler strain."

Once we had moved to the new camp, no one could remember any more words to songs. It was then that Norah Chambers suggested "Why don't we sing music written for piano and orchestra?" and Margaret Dryburgh said, "Let's try," and brought forth the instrumental works by classical composers which she arranged, with Norah's help, into the wondrous vocal orchestra songs of the 1943 Christmas concert.

When fellow-internees clamored for a second concert, the vocal orchestra could have sung the same pieces again. Everyone would have been happy. But Margaret Dryburgh preferred to further search her memory and come up with new classical works, and arrange those for voices. "This way there will again be surprises." Norah also brought forth a few works from her memory. Singers were sometimes able to fill in missing parts. "One of us would hum a melody, and Miss Dryburgh would write it down, as if in shorthand," said Shelagh later. "It went as quickly as that."

Camp diaries are not clear about the exact number of concerts that followed the 1943 Christmas concert. There were probably three or four. We do know that the total number of vocal orchestra compositions was 30. They are listed here in alphabetical order.

Bach	"Jesu, Joy of Man's Desiring"
Barrett	Coronach from *A Highland Lament*
Beethoven	Minuet in G
Beethoven	First Movement from *Moonlight Sonata*
Boughton	"Faery Song" from *The Immortal Hour*
Brahms	Waltz no. 15
Chaminade	Aubade
Chopin	Prelude no. 6
Chopin	Prelude no. 15, "Raindrop"
Chopin	Prelude no. 20, "Funeral March"
Debussy	"Rêverie"
Dvořák	Humoresque no. 7
Dvořák	Largo *From the New World* Symphony
Godard	Berceuse from *Jocelyn*

Grainger	"Country Gardens" (Morris dance tune)
Grieg	"Morning" from *Peer Gynt* Suite no. 1
Handel	*Messiah* pastorale (in Christmas Medley)
MacDowell	"Sea Song"
MacDowell	"To a Wild Rose"
Mendelssohn	"Shepherd's Complaint" from *Songs Without Words*
Mendelssohn	Venetian Gondola Song no. 3
Mozart	Allegro from Sonata in C
Paderewski	"Menuet à l'antique"
Ravel	*Bolero*
Schubert	First Movement from *Unfinished Symphony*
Schumann	"Dreaming" from *Scenes of Childhood*
Tchaikovsky	Andante Cantabile from String Quartet
(Irish)	"Londonderry Air"
(German)	"Shepherd's Dance" from *Henry VIII*
(Scottish)	"Auld Lang Syne"

Each time a concert was presented, a large part of the camp attended, and many dressed up for it—in a long-saved dress, with a ribbon, a borrowed lipstick, or with pre-camp shoes that were uncomfortable to wear on feet more recently used to being bare.

Those who did not attend either were ill or recuperating from having been ill, or were tied up with essential camp duties like nursing. And there were some who just couldn't raise any enthusiasm for this type of music. Mrs. Sargeant Major's fears that the Japanese wouldn't tolerate a concert gathering were unfounded. In fact, at one concert three officers came and sat in crisp uniforms and highly polished boots in rattan chairs in the pendopo while the rest of the audience sat on the ground or stood outside. As a token of appreciation, our captors gave the vocal orchestra five small cans of SPAM to divide between them.

Each time we heard the music we marveled again at the beautiful and often familiar melodies, at the purity of sound, at this miracle that was happening to us amid the cockroaches, the rats, the bedbugs, and the stink of the latrines. The music renewed our sense of human dignity. We had to live under bestial conditions but, by Jove, we could rise above them!

The choir continued to practice in the stuffy shed off the kitchen, always in the evening by the light of one pale, dangling bulb. Often a singer or two were missing because of illness, and sometimes a new face appeared.

With much patience Norah took her motley collection of singers in hand. Some had sung in choirs before the war, had played the piano or violin. They knew about quarter-notes and eighth-notes, they knew the difference between *pianissimo* and *forte*. Others had never sung anything more dramatic than children's ditties and couldn't read music at all. (These held their scores just for looks.) But these novices sat next to a more accomplished singer so they had someone to follow in learning the melodies.

"First we have to get the learning done, actually learning the notes," Norah explained. "Then we start to put in color, I mean light and shade, slow or fast . . . Of course, you have to practice your parts ahead of rehearsal on your own. If you can't read music, ask someone in your section to help you."

"Norah was a hard task master," Antoinette would say years later. "She never let a false note or a muddled phrasing go by. She made us go back again and again, until we got the music just right." She added pensively, "But to sing measure 32 and 33 correctly became very important and took your mind off whether you were hungry, or thirsty, or feeling sick, or just plain down in the dumps."

About the same time I received a letter from Betty Jeffrey in Melbourne who also reminisced, "When I sang that vocal orchestra music, I forgot I was in the camp. I felt free."

Chapter Eleven

Each for Herself?

s 1944 dragged on, we still had no news from the outside world. Conditions in the Palembang barracks camp steadily deteriorated. Rations became even smaller, illnesses increased, and fellow internees began to die.

One of the first was a Sacred Heart nun. I remembered her from the houses camp, a strapping young woman from North Brabant, joking with her Dutch pupils as they sat in a circle on the ground while she taught them the ABC's without books. Now, as I stepped outside to look at the stars, I saw her biered up in the *pendopo*. A sheet covered her body. Other nuns kept vigil, murmuring prayers.

I saw Sigrid and whispered, "What did she die of?"

"I don't really know, but whatever it was, with proper food and medication, she needn't have died. She was only 35."

The compound was conspicuously empty that night. The body under the sheet was a reminder of what could happen to all of us. I returned to my barrack.

Shortly after breakfast the next morning I happened to be near the gate where Mother Laurentia and one of the Sacred Heart nuns were talking to the guard. They wanted to conduct a proper funeral service at the gravesite. But the guard refused permission. He beckoned two other women to carry the sheet-wrapped body from the bier to a truck outside the gate, and the driver pulled away, taking our fellow-prisoner with him. Whether she ever received a coffin and where she was buried, no one in the camp was able to find out.

The small hospital barrack was now always filled with very sick women and children. Some 40 lay on their own mattress pads, under their own nets, on the split-bamboo platforms. They lay squashed together like herrings in a barrel, pestered by fat rats and tireless bedbugs that clung to the nets and spread a thickening smell when pulled off and pinched between thumb and index finger. The accommodations were as abominable as those in the regular barracks, but the sick did receive loving nursing care from the Charitas sisters or from Australian nurses and lay-nurses who pitched in.

To the malaria and dysentery already prevalent in the houses camp was added wet beri-beri, a disease caused by dietary deficiencies: liquid formed under the skin of feet and legs, moved up to the rest of the body and eventually reached the heart. A patient's arm might become so swollen she couldn't bend it to feed herself. If someone stroked her arm, the skin might just peel off.

When statistics were calculated after the war, the death rate at our camp was determined to be 37%. Many died from beri-beri. Doses of vitamin-B could have saved them.

Some of the dead left a will, handwritten on a tiny piece of paper. (If a woman without "heirs" failed to leave a will, the Japanese were likely to confiscate the "estate.") Shelagh told me that one of the English women bequeathed a hairbrush to her. "It's lovely to be able to brush my hair again. It's been more than two years since I did."

More deaths brought more anxiety among us. Who will be next, each one thought. The Japanese didn't give us medicines to combat our illnesses, let alone better food. The only way to stave off death was to build up ourselves by obtaining extra food at the black market, which was again flourishing. But to trade at the black market we needed cash, and by now many more of us had none.

New money-making schemes were hatched. One was the cutting down of Dutch peoples' wide capoc mattresses to fit the new narrow bed spaces on the *balai-balai*. Another strategy, already used at bazaars in the houses camp, was to raffle off prized items, such as a pair of shoes.

I usually bought raffle tickets. A pair of shoes would almost certainly be the wrong size for me; but if I'd won shoes, I could sell them again and buy something else. Or did I buy tickets out of a sense of community spirit, the way I now buy girl scout cookies from the girl next door? Probably not. Generosity became a more and more precious quality in the fight for survival and the choice between "good for others" and "good for ourselves" was the subject of much debate between my sisters and me.

I remember a long discussion we had when Marie, one of our neighbors on the balai-balai, begged us for a little money so she could buy extra food and get her strength back after an illness. Marie had spent money like water during the first year in the camp. She could have been less reckless and saved for a rainy day. We forgot, of course, that Marie, like we girls, never dreamed we would be interned for this long. Also, Marie wasn't doing a spot of work. She was a drone. My sisters and I were workers. It would be important for the community that we maintain the strength we still had. We would spend the money on ourselves.

When we ran out of cash, we joined the money earners. Alette was the first to find a job. She took in laundry for a Dutch mother who lay most of the day on the balai-balai surrounded by four children, who had to stay there, "so I can keep an eye on you." They looked as spotless as it was possible to look in the dirty camp. The oldest was a girl of eight who washed the younger children in the communal bathroom. I'd often seen her mothering the little ones—three stick-thin kids who barely smiled anymore. I called the mother "Mrs. Mean" because she hit the children with a leather belt when they misbehaved on the balai-balai.

Alette did her job early in the morning before she left for kitchen duty. One morning the swish-swoosh of her brush on the washboard aggravated Mrs. Sargeant Major, who woke everyone in the barrack by yelling, "Alette, stop that noise." When Alette went on brushing, Mrs. Sargeant Major crawled out from under her mosquito net, strode over to the well, grabbed the brush from the astonished Alette, and repaired to her net. "She was wearing a nightgown!" Alette reported later. "Imagine still having such a thing."

Not the kind of person to yell back, Alette left, letting the laundry sit at the well. Here it soon became spattered with mud as others came to haul water. Mother Laurentia asked for the brush back later in the day and settled the matter in favor of Alette.

I followed the lead of several other women in the camp by making soup for sale. We had brought our brazier from the houses camp. I had wood scraps—the perks of my wood carrying job. With money Alette put into the "family kitty," I bought *kacang hijau* and salt at the black market and simmered the peas in water. I then sold the soup by the ladle and put money back in the kitty.

"You charge too much for something that's nothing more than water with a little kacang hijau flavor," said Alette once.

"Oh, but my soup is hot," I retorted. "If I don't sell the soup immediately, I always go back to the brazier to reheat it. Besides, I always put salt in it . . . and I do charge the going rate." I continued to go up and down the aisles of the barrack with my tin and ladle crying, "Soup for sale." I was paid now in Japanese paper money that carried the Dutch words *De Japansche Regeering betaalt aan toonder,* "The Japanese government pays to bearer."

Antoinette didn't have a paying job. She was too busy helping Norah Chambers copy music for the members of the vocal orchestra. When Antoinette suggested that she too should earn money to put in the kitty, Alette and I convinced her that there weren't many women able to copy music, and with the general mood growing more somber as conditions worsened, another vocal orchestra concert was of vital importance.

Bartering was another way to obtain food or other means to embellish a dreary camp life.

"I'll give you the warm water I receive for kitchen duty. You give me a yard of thread."

". . . half a coconut shell for a pencil stub."

". . . the use of your needle for the use of my whittling knife."

". . . sugar for tobacco."

Some women would rather roll a cigarette and smoke it than eat food. Others would rather sew and look neat than have a treat. "That little bitty piece of sugar will be gone immediately, but a patch on my dress will last."

Keeping up appearances, not "letting yourself go," was still important in the camp. Few of us wore the ripped and filthy rags shown in postwar films about the Southeast Asia women's camps. By and large, we all set store by sewing patch upon patch and looking "mended" and as clean as possible. Some women, after two years of captivity, still put their shorts under their sleeping pad to "iron" a crease into them while they slept. The "English" kept up their tea rituals, although playing charades and reciting poems were by now just too tiring. One group pitched in money to buy a tablecloth: a tablecloth for tea was chic. Many women refused to lick their plates or bowls, and made sure their children didn't either.

As we were struggling to buoy ourselves up on one hand while being worn down on the other, we all began suffering from another camp disease: "camp irritation." We were getting on each other's nerves.

There were more yells from mothers to children, from neighbor to neighbor on the balai-balai.

"I can't stand to hear you practicing for that orchestra," someone hurled at Antoinette, who was softly humming the accompaniment for a vocal orchestra piece.

"Hey, you there, your son is really too big to suck his thumb."

"Don't give her sugar for breakfast. It will only make her diarrhea worse."

"The whole balai-balai shakes when you turn around. Turn around more carefully!"

Antoinette, Alette, and I, soft-spoken, well-mannered young girls when we entered camp, were now shrieking at each other. Sometimes there was a solution to a quarrel, as with the individual rations of sugar, salt, or palm oil. First we kept these precious provisions together—three portions in each container. But we could never agree on their use. Use it today? Save it for tomorrow? Enjoy it all at once? A drop at a time? As soon as we managed to obtain more empty tins, we each established our own tins of sugar, salt, and palm oil. But other quarrels lingered on and on. And these would eventually lead to a break-up of our *kongsi* of three.

The original cooking kongsis continued to exist after cooking was taken over by the community kitchen. Kongsi members took care of each other. Particularly strong were the kongsis of Margaret Dryburgh and others who lived in the garage of house number 9 in the houses camp; of the Australian nurses, a homogeneous group welded by army discipline and by a common professional background; and of the three groups of nuns, trained in the disciplines of monastic life. Other kongsi's dissolved or re-grouped with the move to the barracks camp. Or they fell apart, as my family's kongsi did.

Once all the camp chores were done, gossip about each other became the chief activity in the camp. One topic that kept tongues wagging involved two women who shared a mosquito net. I was too naive to understand the knowing winks and the snickering innuendoes. Not until years later, when homosexuality became a household word, did I begin to wonder whether the twosome had perhaps been lesbians. I doubt it. Reports on women's internment camps and prisoner of war camps reveal that prisoners who were starved and weakened by disease, as those two women were, generally lost interest in sex. They probably shared one net for the purely practical reason that between them they didn't have enough netting for two. Or they were in need of friendship and camaraderie, as the rest of us were, and satisfied each other's need to be "fussed over," as Shelagh once put it. Shelagh wasn't thinking of sex when she said that.

However, in our camp, there were a few Eurasian women whom we called "girlfriends," who clearly retained an interest in sex. They were not yet starved and weakened by disease: they received extras from their Japanese "hosts." That some of them may have gone visiting because they *needed* the extras for themselves or their children didn't often occur to us in the beginning of captivity. To be friendly with the enemy seemed unbelievably despicable behavior. In due time the criticisms of the girlfriends lost their sharp edges. The women were even grudgingly praised: some shared the food they "earned" with fellow-internees.

One such woman was a Eurasian I called Mrs. Lily Leaf. When she walked, her still-ample behind wiggled like a lily leaf in a wind-rippled pond. "White, brown, or yellow, it makes no difference. It is my profession," she is rumored to have said to Mother Laurentia, as the two were discussing who among the Dutch families should receive the extra foods Mrs. Lily Leaf had given to Mother Laurentia to distribute.

However, most extra food that came into the camp arrived via the *gedék* trade. This was the black market conducted through a hole in the gedék, the plaited bamboo wall of the camp. Food obtained this way had to be paid for—dearly. A gold ring might pay for 3 duck eggs and a chili pepper.

The camp's go-betweens were Eurasian women who spoke Malay fluently and, being part Asian, related better to the Asians on the other side of the fence than any of the purely Dutch or British internees. These go-betweens were not friendly with the Japanese.

"The queen of them all," Dutch Saartje told me a few years ago, "was Nel. Do you remember her?"

"Sure, she sang in the vocal orchestra."

"With her dark skin and dressed in black, she honestly was just a shadow at night. I mean, you couldn't even see her."

Saartje then told me this story:

"One of the Dutch women had a clock to sell. When you leave your home, you grab things. I don't really know why she did such a silly thing as grabbing that clock. But, of course, I had only one teeny bag, and what I put into that bag was absolutely idiotic. Nothing like a toothbrush or a comb or anything like that. So she had a clock, a lovely little Swiss thing, very beautiful. It played a little minuet. She brought it to Nel and played it. It was out of this world. That tinkly, lovely, pure sound. Of course, we thought it much more beautiful than we would now. Anyway, we played it and played it, and Nel said that the Chinese on the outside would love it. She took it on consignment. But before handing the clock over, the owner had wound it again, forgetting it would start playing after some time. Nel was all in black. She crept toward the gedék to meet her outside contact, and the clock started to play. Nel ran back to her *tempat*, put the clock inside her clothes, put it across her stomach, pulled up her knees, hugged it, but the clock wouldn't stop until it had played itself out. Nel escaped being caught."

The black market trade was a risky business. We all remembered the Chinese man who had been tied up and left to die in the houses camp because he had sold us loaves of bread over the barbed-wire fence. Such thoughts raised the question of whether it was fair to expose the go-betweens to the risks of punishment and, most likely, torture. But, so went the arguments, the go-betweens didn't *have* to serve in that way. They could stop running the risk at any time. And, for those of us who placed orders with them, the extra food we received could mean the difference between life and death. So the black market continued—and our consciences alternately clouded and cleared.

One day, in the midst of our growing nutritional crisis, the Japanese announced that we had to grow *ubi kayu*, or cassava, in the compound. Cries of protest went up, carried to the Japanese by Mother Laurentia, and Dr. McDowell's successor, Mrs. Gertrude Hinch, the American wife of an English principal of an Anglo-Chinese Methodist school in Singapore. We were in the dry season, they pointed out, and the ground was as hard as bricks. It was true we needed food, but we also needed all the walking space we could get. In our minds, the idea of giving over that precious space to back-breaking cultivation cancelled out the minimal food value we could expect from the cassavas. Naturally, such arguments achieved nothing. With dust blowing in our faces and sweat trickling down our backs, we chiseled furrows in the ground with mattocks. To the representatives' complaints that those mattocks were too heavy for us in our weakened condition, the guard replied that Japanese women had to work hard, too.

Next, we had to water the young plants with gorgeous clear water from a tap outside the camp. As a guard watched, long lines of women and children carrying buckets, tins, and pans had to draw the water from the tap and carry the containers back to pour it over the cassavas. Nothing seemed so unfair to us as having to throw that beautiful water over the cassavas, while we had to bathe ourselves out of a five-pound butter tin filled with brackish water drawn from the near-empty well. Once a woman was caught smuggling this beautiful clean water into the barrack. The guard saw it and beat her face bloody.

In watering the ubi kayus, we could at least dream of the day when we would eat them. However, we also had to carry fresh water from this tap to Japanese officers' houses and fill their bathroom basins so they could take those refreshing "splash baths" we longed for. This was a grim job, yet the number of volunteers for it always exceeded the Japanese quota. After all, this job took workers outside the camp, if only briefly, making it a "perk" like no other. Also, a water carrier could hold a bucket with clean water on her shoulder, "accidentally" spill it over herself, and so have a lovely bath. In the face of such delectable treats, it was easy to ignore the true object of the water-carrying effort.

As a group—"English" and Dutch alike—we became wily and shrewd. Betty Jeffrey reports in her diary, printed after the war, how a squad of internees was sent to remove a garbage heap 400 yards along a road to the back garden of a house where the Japanese guards slept. The women pretended not to understand the instructions of their guard, who was sitting a distance away in the shade, and they piled the stinking rubbish right under the window. The group derived much pleasure from imagining the full aroma of the garbage heated by the midday sun wafting into the house.

Another time, according to Jeff's diary:

> Loony the Dill produced a lawn mower and instructed a couple of our girls on how to use it. They had to mow a lawn of an officer's house. Their effort was amusing, starting with a frightened look at the little mower and muttering, "*Apa*?"—Malay for "What is that?"
>
> Loony told them in Malay not to be worried and showed them how to use the mower. He ran it up and down a strip of lawn. The girls knew how to block the mower, and did so, then sat down in the shade and waited for him to come back. He came soon, and they told him it was stuck. He unstuck it and did two more strips to show them how easy it was, then handed the thing over to them. He went away once more, and once more they jammed it and went off and sat down. Again poor Loony came to their aid. He still hasn't realized he cut the whole lawn.

In April 1944, a change in Japanese authorities who ran the camp brought about subtle changes. Every month we were to be weighed. This filled us with hope. When the Japanese noticed that our weights were dropping every month, they would increase our rations. They did no such thing; they stopped the weighing.

We also began to receive shots against cholera and typhoid. Some women said this meant that Japan was finally adhering to the rules of the Geneva Convention governing the treatment of prisoners of war: captors are to take care of captives' health. My personal belief was that the Japanese wanted to prevent an epidemic among the prisoners because they were worried about their own health. In the camp we discovered that a sure way to keep a guard away was to cough and say you had tuberculosis.

For a short while we received a monthly allowance, and a vendor was allowed into the camp again to sell us extra food. But our regular rations remained as meager and unnourishing as ever.

During this period, the first Red Cross parcels arrived. For more than two years we had waited anxiously to receive such packages, wondering with growing alarm whether anyone in the world was aware of our plight as prisoners.

The parcels were marked AMERICAN RED CROSS. We could see them through cracks in the gedék fence. But it was two weeks before the Japanese let the parcels into the camp. By that time the guards had eaten most of our chocolate bars and smoked most of our cigarettes. But the powdered milk, sugar, canned meat, processed cheese, and canned butter that did come in, even though individual portions were small, helped in the continuing battle against physical decline. The psychological benefits of the shipment were enormous. As I recall, it was the only shipment we received.

In August 1944, the first Red Cross cards also came. They had been written two years before. What had kept them so long? The cards were written in either Malay or English, presumably a Japanese requirement, and the 25 words allowed were vague and noncommittal: the writers were all doing fine, and telling their loved ones not to worry about them.

Camp emotions about the cards were mixed.

"How do I know my mother is *still* in good health."

"Oh, to see Mother's handwriting, even if it is two years old, makes me so happy."

"Well, at least I know now I am an aunt."

"He doesn't say where he is, just that he is in a prisoner-of-war camp."

Ruth received the long-awaited card from her husband. He was a prisoner in Singapore's Changi jail.

Many of us received no cards. My sisters and I did not. Later we admitted to each other that we had been worried sick that there was no card from Mother. Did this mean she was not alive?

Women in the camp construed the Red Cross parcels and the cards as good signs, along with the SPAM for the vocal orchestra singers. The Japanese must be losing the war and were eager to make a good impression before surrender. But when the Japanese were downright awful, we also construed that as a good sign. The Japanese were losing the war and were now taking their anger and frustration out on us. We capped these airy speculations with that eternal bit of camp optimism, "The war will surely be over in six months."

Nothing could have given us more hope than the bombs that fell on the night of August 11, 1944, on nearby Pladju. Before the Japanese occupation, the BPM had pumped and refined oil there and stored it in huge tanks. The Dutch had partially destroyed the installations before the invasion, but the Japanese repaired them and were operating the facility again at full speed, as we later learned.

The wail of air raid sirens, the ack-ack-ack of anti-aircraft guns, the bomb blasts, the fires in the distance, they were reminiscent of Japanese air attacks on Singapore and Batavia. No one doubted that the planes dropping the bombs now were Allied planes. The sounds were "like the voices of angels," someone said. We were all gathered in the compound. "This is even better than vocal orchestra music," said another. We still were looking deliriously at the night sky from whence these hopeful sounds came when the guard came running out of the guardhouse and chased us inside.

A few days later the Allied planes again dropped bombs on Pladju, and we talked excitedly about what this could mean for us. Then silence reigned again above the camp. No planes flew over. No anti-aircraft guns were fired off. Camp life returned to its dreary dullness, and we talked again about who had quarreled with whom and who was shirking her part in the community work.

♥ ♥ ♥

A few weeks later we had to pack for another move. We would be sent away from Sumatra to Muntok on the island of Bangka, which lies off Sumatra's southeast coast. We would be near our men again, but the move would mean building a new "home" in the next camp. Although this was only our second move, we had already learned to "be happy with what you have, because you don't know what you'll get."

Most of us saw the move as a great sign: We were being moved because an Allied landing was imminent. The Japanese wanted us out of the way, so we wouldn't be there to lend the Allies a helping hand.

I fell for this reasoning, too. It was a stab in the dark, of course, but we had to hang on to something. I created in my mind a happy scene of the three of us girls seeing Father again and celebrating the end of the war together with Mother, who had joined us from somewhere.

Surely, Muntok would be our last camp.

Chapter Twelve

Second Barracks Camp: Burials

Creaking and groaning, the little Bangka-bound steamer heaved up and down. Huge waves swept over the deck, where a group of us clutched each other and held onto our precious belongings.

"Don't move about," the Japanese guard had shouted in Malay when the storm started. "The ship is old!" We couldn't have moved if we had tried, pressed together as we were.

Seasick women and children vomited into an empty tin that was passed from hand to hand and emptied into the sea.

A Japanese guard produced a helmet to serve as chamberpot. Once in awhile, with a single such gesture a Japanese would emerge from the great mass of "the enemy" and plant himself in my memory as an actual human being. The pot was emptied in the same way as the vomit tin.

Every time a wave was about to wash over us, one of the Charitas sisters, on deck with patients from the camp hospital, cried, "Here she comes." Then the nuns would reach over the sick and push them against the deck. When the water receded, the nuns' white habits clung to their bodies and revealed their bony hips and flat bosoms.

"I've been saving a piece of *gula jawa*," said Antoinette who sat next to me. "This is a good time to eat it." She rummaged among our tins in the woven-grass bag for one with her name on it.

"I'm going to save my sugar for later," I said.

"If you think you are going to be seasick, too, you'd better. If not, I'd take some sugar now. You're going to need the energy."

I took a piece out of my tin.

The storm abated, and the little boat steamed on toward our next prison camp.

I thought about the past turbulent weeks. The Japanese had sent in a hundred or so women and children from a camp in Bengkulen to go with us to Bangka. I was delighted to see Mrs. Herrebrugh and her three children, whom I had met two-and-half years before in Krui, at the beginning of our captivity. But all these Bengkulen people had to be accommodated in our barracks. Our sleeping spaces on the *balai-balai*'s narrowed again.

In preparation for the journey, the new total of 700 internees in the Palembang barracks camp was divided into three groups, each to depart at a different time. When the first group was told to be ready, they pulled the mosquito-net nails out of the barrack poles, packed the nails and their belongings, and stood ready at the appointed time, only to be informed that they would not be moved for another week. They unpacked everything again and hammered the nails back in. Eventually, this group left, carrying portions of cooked rice from the community kitchen to eat en route.

When the second group (my group) left, the kitchen had been unable to prepare food to eat during the transport, and the Japanese didn't provide any either.

As we steamed down the River Musi toward its estuary and the open sea where the storm caught us, I had let my legs and feet dangle out of the boat. It was lovely to feel the hot wind against my bare skin. Near Palembang women washed their laundry in the river. Men paddled flat sampans with fruits and vegetables. How comforting it was to realize that life outside the camp was proceeding normally.

For the children on the little boat, the trip was an enormous adventure.

"Look at those trees moving," a child near me cried.

"Yes, the wind does that," the mother said.

Nothing at all grew in the barracks camp we had just left—except the *ubi kayu's* we had had to plant in the compound. We had to abandon them without having had the joy of eating any of them.

"Look at that beast with a tail under the chin," said another child, pointing to a scrawny village goat along the shore.

Later in the morning the swaying trees along the shore gave way to mangrove bushes, their aerial roots sticking grotesquely into the air. Beyond the mangroves stretched swamps, green and monotonous as far as the eye could see. Now the only signs of human habitation were grey painted boats flying the white flag with the fiery red ball. Soldiers milled about on deck in loin cloths.

"Oh Mama, they're wearing diapers," shouted a little girl gleefully. The mother was annoyed and said, "Don't look at them. They are Japanese soldiers." Their bare buttocks were fat, not skin-over-bones like ours.

Late in the evening our boat docked at the planked pier of Muntok. It was a long pier to walk, 600 meters long, and had no railings that I can remember, only water on both sides that shimmered in the moonlight and was also visible through large cracks between the planks.

The hospital nuns and the sick were ordered off the boat first. At the end of the pier, Japanese soldiers stood ready with real stretchers (not our kind made from bamboo poles and rice sacks that sagged in the middle) to transfer the sick to a truck marked with a large red cross. At first, I thought the truck belonged to the International Red Cross, that the outside world had finally discovered us. But the truck was Japanese. My sisters and I joined the second group ordered off the boat and trudged down the pier in a long line of women and children loaded down with bedrolls, bundles of clothing, woven-grass bags, an odd suitcase, a pair of shoes or *terompah's* around the neck, tins and coconut shells dangling from an arm. Each adult or child carried all she owned.

In the new camp, women from the first group had prepared steaming rice for us. But the Japanese didn't want us to eat it. We were shooed to the barracks, and had to wait until the next day to eat cold rice.

These barracks had just been built, allowing each person about twice as much living space on the balai-balai as in the previous camp. There also was more walking space between and around the six long barracks, which paralleled each other. One barrack was taken up by the community kitchen and community bathing area and latrines, and part of another was designated the camp hospital. Water again had to be drawn from wells, and in this camp there was no electricity.

The "English" and the Dutch again were lodged by nationality, but this time my sisters moved into one of the English barracks to be with friends from the vocal orchestra. Recently the three of us tried to reconstruct the reasons for the break-up of our *kongsi* . But we couldn't come up with much, other than that I probably was too motherly, doing too much of my "big-sister-thing," and the girls had to show some independence. And, of course, there was the "camp irritation." I became a kongsi of one in a Dutch barrack not far from the Carolus Borromeus nuns. At this time I did not want to be in another kongsi; I just wanted to be by myself.

We all were cheered by the new surroundings. A camp with more space, more fresh air, and trees and greenery to see beyond the barbed-wire fence, as in the houses camp. But very soon what we called "Bangka fever" began to rage through our camp. Sufferers ran high temperatures for days on end, lost consciousness, and died. This illness was probably a form of cerebral malaria.

And the cases of beri-beri increased. One camp child remembers how she pressed her finger on her mother's swollen leg and the pressure left a red mark that wouldn't go away. Then she knew that her mother had beri-beri and likely was to die. Another camp child remembers going to our own "Red Cross office," and asking for one of the "Red Cross blankets" (blanket left by internees who had died), "because my mommy has the malaria shivers," and having this same fear of losing her mother.

Before our internment was over, 26 Dutch children lost their mothers and were taken in by the Sisters of Carolus Borromeus.

Sometimes the camp deaths were just statistics, "two more in barrack number 1," or "a mother in barrack number 3 lost a boy today, and she had already lost a girl last week." Sometimes the deaths were women I knew, Shelagh's mother, an Australian nurse I had befriended at soirees in the houses camp, and Ruth with whom I had walked with in the houses camp and carried wood and daydreamed with in the Palembang barracks camp.

Almost without exception, these deaths were due to tropical diseases and starvation. Some of the sick tried valiantly to stay alive. Others, hit by the dreaded "camp lethargy" (that no amount of ecncouragement from friends could dispel), simply gave up.

The call for grave diggers had gone through the camp. I was standing at the wooden gate of the barbed-wire fence with another woman and Marianne, a Dutch girl. She was 15 now but with her thin, tired face she looked years older.

"You here again?" I said to Marianne.

"Yes, I always volunteer. Gives me a chance to get away from that barrack."

One of the Australian nurses joined us. We waited for the guard to come out of the little palm-frond-covered hut next to the gate. The three others and I, standing uncomfortably in the hot sun, speculated on how many graves we would have to dig. We knew that two women had died that morning. So that made two graves, at least. Some weeks before the guard had ordered the squad to dig eight graves, although fewer than eight people had died. What if the guard today was planning for future deaths? We were so weak now that the idea of digging two graves already seemed dreadful. Please, no extra ones!

When a stake truck stopped before the gate, the guard came out of his office carrying four mattocks. We grave diggers made the required bow and were each handed a mattock. We walked toward the truck and up the lowered tailgate.

The driver was a Bangka man. He stuck his head out from the cab, apparently not afraid of the Japanese guard, and told us in Malay that he had been to the nearby men's camp and that many men had died there as well. This was no news. Just yesterday our two camp representatives had been given a list with names of Dutch and British men who had died in the men's camp. I had seen Mother Laurentia walk down my barrack to tell a woman near me that her husband's name was on the list.

I had hardly been able to breathe when I saw Mother Laurentia talk to my neighbor. Would she stop next at my bedspace and tell me that Father had died? But she had gone off in the other direction. So Father's name had not been on the list. But how current was that list anyway? Maybe Father had died since the list was compiled? I had tried to reassure myself about Father. He had been in tip-top physical condition at the beginning of captivity. With his many years of mountaineer training and his explorations of the jungles and high mountains of the world, he was used to hard, physical work and to coping with rigorous conditions. He surely would be better able to adjust to the rigors of camp life than some fat, lazy man who had spent his life in the colonies sitting around in wicker chairs drinking whiskey.

The truck continued its bumpy route over the potholed dirt road to the cemetery, and I thought again about the death lists. Why were the Japanese torturing us this way, allowing only news of deaths to come into the camp? Surely permitting a few notes to pass back and forth between the living would not hamper the progress of the Japanese war? We were so close to our husbands and fathers here at Bangka, and yet no exchange of letters, no visits. . .

The frustration was excruciating, in a way made even keener by a one-time exception to the rule. A few of the boys who had been sent to the men's camp two years before suddenly appeared near our camp. Unaccountably, the Japanese had given them permission to ride with the ration truck that delivered food to the men and afterward to the women's camp. We were taken completely by surprise when the cry, "Our boys!" went through the camp. Whose sons would be there? One of them was Theo, quoted earlier. After the war, Theo recalled the scene. "We saw the women's camp, and there was barbed wire, and we were standing five meters on this side, and suddenly my mother was there on the other side . . . with three of my brothers still. Later I heard that when she knew that we were there, she quickly dressed up and tried to get a sort of long skirt on to hide her beri-beri legs, and to hide that she was fully emaciated by that time. It was only a matter of two minutes. You could hardly speak, you could only wave a little. Then we had to get on to that truck again. And that was the end. Because three months later, she died."

We rumbled on toward the cemetery.

The Australian nurse broke the silence, saying, "At our Sister Raymont's funeral, two Japanese stood at attention and removed their caps as we went past the guardhouse, something they have never done before." The nurses, all wearing their uniforms, had given Ray a military funeral. I had seen them lined up at the gate, standing still and straight, conveying a sense of pride and spunk despite their haggard appearance and the oil stains on their wrinkled grey dresses.

The truck stopped, and we walked up the little knoll to the graves. I saw more crosses than the last time I had been up there. Women in the camp nailed two pieces of wood together and burned in the names with hot nails.

The guard held up two fingers. Two graves only. That was good. He marked off two rectangles with the heel of his boot and indicated that Marianne and I were to dig one grave and the Dutch woman and the Australian were to start on the other.

It had rained a lot in the last few days, so the soil was malleable, but my mattock seemed heavier than ever. I put both hands around the handle, lifted the tool to chest height, and swung it forward into the red, sucking clay. I wrestled the mattock out of the soil. A clump of clay stuck to the blade. I shook the clump off. I lifted the mattock, swung it forward, dug into the soil . . . over and over. Sometimes I had to pause to wait for my heart to stop racing or for a blackout to pass, always hoping the guard wouldn't see that I had stopped and angrily cry "*Lekas, lekas,*" quickly, quickly. But he was snoozing in the shade of a tree.

I wished again that the Japanese would issue us spades to dig the graves instead of these clumsy mattocks. How many times had Mother Laurentia and Mrs. Hinch asked for spades? Surely there must be some on Bangka.

Marianne and I silently toiled away until the time came that one of us had to climb inside the grave and shovel the clay from the bottom up and out. I offered to go.

"I think it's creepy to get in," said Marianne.

"I'm getting used to it," I said, but that wasn't true. I also thought it was creepy.

As I scooped up clay and threw it over the dirt wall building up around the shallow grave, I pictured my own funeral. Would my coffin be long enough? The Japanese provided flimsy, orange-crate-type coffins that often were too short, so that those who put the body inside had to wriggle it into the box. What would I be wearing? It was tempting for those left behind to bury the dead unclothed, since clothes were so scarce in the camp. When nuns were buried in their full habits, women in the communal bathroom, which served as a kind of public square, murmured to each other, "What a pity. Think of all that material disappearing forever," or

"The nuns could have sold that cloth and earned money for their ever-growing family." If I died, I probably would not be buried in my going-away dress. Antoinette and Alette would be able to sell it.

And who would say my funeral service? Sister Catharinia, because she was Dutch and a friend? But she was a Catholic and I was a Protestant. She would only know the Catholic funeral service, though she might lead everyone at the gravesite in the Lord's Prayer. I wouldn't mind if the nuns sang *In paradisum deducant te Angeli*, "The Angels take you to Paradise," as they did for Catholic burials. I liked that Gregorian chant. It seemed special and exotic among the palm trees and tropical vegetation of Bangka. If Sister Catharinia didn't say a few words at my graveside, who would? One of my sisters, no doubt, even though they had "moved out of the house."

What name would someone burn on the cross? Helen Colijn or Helen C. Colijn? I had always found that C. for Constantia a nuisance. I felt I had to live up to it. Had I lived up to it in the camp?

But why was I thinking about my own death? If I still had enough strength to dig a grave, I would have enough strength to hang onto life. As camp health went, I still was in relatively good condition. The ever-recurring malaria attacks were draining, particularly after we used up the supply of quinine pills that Father had bought for us after the shipwreck. But the malaria wasn't as bad as Bangka fever or beri-beri or long bouts of dysentery. There was much to live for. Nearby, in the men's camp, Father was waiting for a joyful reunion with us. Somewhere on Borneo, Mother was waiting to join us when the war was finally over. I would lead a normal life again, go to a university, hike in the mountains or along a beach. Somewhere down the line would be love and marriage and children.

I continued my musings with the thought that surely the end of the war must be near. That's why we were sent to Bangka, wasn't it? The Japanese feared an Allied invasion of Sumatra. Surely three years was enough time for the Americans and other Allies to beat the Japanese. And I had my fantasy again of soldiers coming and swinging open the gates of the camp, shouting, "The war is over, you're free!" Our men would come from the men's camp, and Father would hug the three of us, crying, "Bravissimo!"

"Bravissimo," he had wired from his office in The Hague to Mother, Antoinette, and me when, in 1938, we had climbed France's Mont Blanc, the highest mountain in Europe. I saw myself on top of that peak. Breathing was difficult. My feet were numb with cold, in spite of woolen socks over my boots. The wind was so strong I was afraid our entire party, roped up behind a guide, would be blown off the narrow snow- and ice-covered ridge. On Tarakan Mother had admitted she would have been just as glad to stay in the Chamonix hotel with Alette (at eleven considered too young for the ascent) and to watch our progress up the mountain through a valley telescope, but "someone had to chaperone Helen and Antoinette." Afterward, Father had had a huge bouquet of red roses sent to Mother in the hotel.

Antoinette had been 16 when she climbed Mont Blanc, about the age of Marianne, who was digging a grave with me on Bangka. Marianne, like Alette, was concerned about her schooling. "I just was doing so nicely in school, going from grade to grade," she had told me. "And now the whole thing is interrupted. It will be difficult to catch up."

"I think you should get out now, Helen. The grave is deep enough to hold a coffin."

I climbed out. The other two women also had finished digging. We awoke the guard and boarded the truck.

Back in camp we saw the funeral party waiting to return with two coffins to the burial site.

The next day I had a chance to go outside the camp again, but this time as part of my regular job as a member of the latrine squad. Each morning, two or three pairs of women on a rotating basis stirred up the latrines with coconut shells attached to long bamboo poles, as had been done in the previous camp, and ladled the feces and the creeping, crawling maggots into wooden buckets. Each pair of women then suspended a bucket from a bamboo shoulder pole and carried it past the guard to dump the contents in the bushes outside the camp.

No guard came along on these outings. No other women were around. Just after the sun came up, the air was cool. Little flowers grew below the bushes. We always picked some, perhaps for decorating a coffin. Once I saw a hibiscus in bloom and picked one of the fiery red blossoms to put behind my ear. What I liked most of all was seeing the colorful butterflies. We never saw them inside the camp.

I had volunteered for the latrine job because it afforded the opportunity to leave camp and enjoy the flowers and the butterflies. The job also netted money: latrine workers were paid. This raised eyebrows in the camp. A tin of hot water, the payment for this job in the previous camp, was O.K. But to pay out cash to latrine workers . . . ? This had never been done for a community job before.

The arrangement had been thought up by the camp committee. It had proven nearly impossible to draw enough volunteers for the job. However, we still had our "hearts," the women who complained of a bad heart or other ailment and refused to do any community work, (though they seemed no worse off than anyone else), and some of the hearts still had cash. They would not be further pressured to participate in community chores, but would instead pay into a newly established latrine fund to pay workers. The hearts could think of "farming out" a community job, just as they farmed out their personal laundry or their haircuts. This was the rare solution that "made everyone happy" in the camp. The hearts were off the hook. With money earned, latrine workers were able to buy extras at the black market.

It wasn't just the hearts who were short on community spirit now. In the struggle for survival, other women who in previous years had cheerfully pitched in when a call for volunteers went out now were so weak and numbed by the day-to-day tedium and seemingly endless captivity that they withdrew into themselves. Their horizons narrowed to their own places on the balai-balai, and perhaps to those of persons physically or emotionally close, like kongsi members. They could not muster any energy or thought for those further removed.

On the other hand, some women still were able to include a whole barrack, or even the whole camp, within the scope of their concern. Women who could barely walk themselves went up and down the barracks to talk to the bed-ridden sick for whom there was no room in the camp hospital. These women made sure that the sick took the precious pills that the camp representatives had lately been able to wheedle out of the guards. Some patients had such a craving for cigarettes that they would even exchange the pills for tobacco. Or, patients suffering from the "camp lethargy" simply couldn't be bothered anymore to take medication.

Other great-hearted women were the cooks, who rose early every day to start the kitchen fires, and the Australian nurses, who worked in the camp hospital with the Charitas sisters. Among these was a dedicated nun who took as her special job the daily washing of the bandages and dressings and the few sheets the hospital recently had inherited.

Another team of women who were still reaching out were the two talented musicians Margaret Dryburgh and Norah Chambers. Although some of the singers had died, the vocal orchestra sang in the hospital barrack around Christmas 1944. It was the last of the "beautifications of life" we had worked on so hard in the previous two camps. After more singers died, the vocal orchestra sang no more.

"But for the surviving singers, the music had become a part within them, and they could at least listen to it and be comforted by it when the camp was quiet at night," Antoinette said recently. "And those who went to the vocal orchestra concerts must have found comfort in the memories of those joyful and uplifting events."

If the starvation-diet and the debilitating diseases dulled our senses, it was perhaps a natural safety valve to help us cope. When we heard of a friend who had died, we could not grieve as we would have in normal times. When Alette came to tell me that Antoinette had gone to the camp hospital with the dreaded Bangka fever, I was not as distraught as I would have been before the war if I had been told my 24-year-old sister was seriously ill, and, as Alette told me, had the color of death. This was a grey-yellowish color on a patient's face that usually heralded that the end was near.

I went to see Antoinette every day with soup I made. Several times patients near her gave up the struggle, but Antoinette hung on and the color of death left her face.

She was just regaining a bit of strength in March of 1945 when news came that we all had to go back to Palembang. From there we would go to a place deep inland called Lubuklinggau to be interned on a rubber plantation called Belalau.

This time most of us were too weary to speculate about why the Japanese were moving us, or to come up with reasons for optimism. We just packed and submitted to being transported for the third time.

A camp child with a history his very own was Isidore Warman (erroneously called Misha in the camp). Having lost both parents in the sinking of the *Vyner Brooke* and its aftermath, he was lovingly cared for by Margaret Dryburgh and other members of her *kongsi*. He is shown here in 1945 at age six en route to England with one of his "camp mothers." He was later reunited with relatives in Shanghai, and now lives in California. Of his three-and-a-half years internment on Sumatra he remembers nothing at all.

Chapter Thirteen

Third Barracks Camp: Release

"All I remember of that trip to Belalau is that the the two women next to me died," Antoinette was to say of the three-day journey to our fourth camp. She traveled in the stretcher transport with others who were very weak or very ill.

Four other patients did not make it. The accompanying Charitas and Australian sisters had to close two coffins at the Muntok pier and four at railroad stations on Sumatra and leave them behind for burial at sites unknown. The Japanese had sent empty coffins along in anticipation of deaths.

I also remember little of the transport to Belalau. Even shortly after the war, when I wrote an account of my internment, much of this voyage was a blur. Alette was in a different group. This time the crossing of Bangka Straits was calm, so no one was seasick. In the train from Palembang to Lubuklinggau we were packed into a cattle car with the doors tightly closed for most of the 48-hour journey. The stench of sweat, urine, and excrement was terrible. We were given no food or water. But after arriving by truck in Belalau, we could walk among the rubber trees and enjoy the sight of flowering alamanda bushes.

It turned out that our men had also been moved from Bangka and were at the other end of the rubber plantation. It was inoperative now: the Dutch had destroyed the rubber-pressing machinery as part of the scorched-earth policy.

My sisters and I felt comforted that Father was nearby again even if the Japanese still prohibited all communication between the camps. Our only news of the men came in the form of the death lists the Japanese delivered to Mother Laurentia and Mrs. Hinch.

Antoinette was released from the camp hospital barrack, one similar to the other barracks with the usual aisle flanked by split-bamboo *balai-balai*'s, but this time the roofs were made of corrugated iron and didn't leak. She returned to her job in the community kitchen, where Alette also worked. The girls were still "rooming" elsewhere, and most of the time we met, we merely gave each other a small sign of recognition or a tired little wave. That's all we were able to muster up for each other.

Looking back on the Belalau camp, I remember mostly a zombie-like existence. I lived in a vacuum, a kind of holding pattern between life and death. I did what I was supposed to do. I carried wood, fetched food in the community kitchen, occasionally made and sold soup of black-market ingredients. I lay on my *tempat* a lot. Sometimes I swatted cockroaches or deloused a neighbor's hair as she deloused mine.

We can't all have been zombies, though, because a few months before the end at least one group was still singing. Antoinette saved a chit of paper from which it is clear that in June 1945 a three-voice glee choir sang (among other songs) "The Keel Row" (As I came thro Sandgate I heard a lassie sing), the Barcarolle from *The Tales of Hoffman*, and "Drink to Me Only" (With Thine Eyes). And Betty Jeffrey wrote in her diary on August 17, 1945, "There is always something to laugh at and talk about, but we are really very tired of this life here."

What I remember most vividly of the camp was the increased sense of isolation. We now were nearly 400 kilometers away from Palembang, with dense jungle surrounding us. Was anyone going to find us here when the war was over? What was happening in the war, anyway? We hadn't heard any rumors for ages, let alone authentic news.

In the spring of 1945, the Allied armies pressed across Europe and pushed the Germans back. Hitler shot himself in a Berlin bunker. Mussolini's body was hanged upside down in a Milan square. Roosevelt died. The Japanese sustained severe losses in the Pacific. But among the rubber trees in Belalau, we knew none of this. We discussed people's last words, and what they had left, and who had inherited.

"What, Beryl didn't get Ann's sugar? And she took such good care of Ann when she was sick. I don't think it's fair of our Red Cross committee to give the sugar to Joan. I know Joan needs it more than Beryl. But, after all, Beryl did nurse Ann."

"You'll be amazed to hear this, they found some quinine pills in Ann's bag."

"For goodness sake, why didn't she take them for her malaria?"

"She must have saved the pills to sell and buy food."

It was hard to know what was more important for survival, food or medicine. Some said food, and bartered or sold anything, including pills, for something extra to eat. Others said medicine, and bartered or sold anything to obtain pills.

❧   ❧   ❧

On April 21, 1945 we lost Miss Dryburgh.

She never recovered after falling ill during the transport to Belalau, "a ghastly journey," as she described it in her diary. "I had to be transferred to the stretcher carriage [of the train.]"

This was her last entry. When parts of Margaret Dryburgh's diary were privately published after the war, Norah Chambers added:

> She was taken into the hospital and should have recovered, but like all the others was so weak that she just couldn't. When I went to see her she was semi-conscious. She recognized me and tried to speak. After a struggle, I found that she was trying to say her favorite psalm, the twenty-third. I stumbled through it, to the best of my ability. Then there was a silence. Suddenly, in a strong voice, and with a smile, she said, 'That's what I wanted.' She passed away shortly afterwards. I helped to bury her and before the coffin was closed put a bunch of flowers in her hands. She looked so peaceful and content, for she had done her job and done it well. Her grave was marked by a simple wooden cross. We planted some flowers

and a big alamanda at her head, as she always loved flowers so much.

Some camp funerals were attended only by the women who had volunteered to carry the coffin and the Dutch or English camp representative, who went by virtue of her position. Miss Dryburgh's funeral was attended by all the members of the vocal orchestra who could walk up the hill to the cemetery, by women of her old *kongsi* in garage number 9 in the houses camp, by women who had picked rice with her in the Palembang barracks camp or who had attended her Bible classes or the Sunday services she occasionally led, and by women who didn't know her personally but had enjoyed the vocal orchestra concerts.

A few days after Miss Dryburgh's funeral, Mother Laurentia stood at the entrance of my barrack and, unable to recognize anyone in the dark inside, asked, "Is Helen Colijn here?"

I knew why she had come. I couldn't even say, "Yes, I am."

The woman stretched out next to me on the balai-balai said, "Yes, she is here."

Slowly, I sat up. When Mother Laurentia reached my bedspace, I said, "I guess our turn has come?"

"Yes, I am afraid so."

"When did he die?"

"On March 11th."

"But the men were still on Bangka then!"

"Yes, he died on Bangka."

"You mean he never was in Belalau . . . ?"

"No, he never was.

"I have something to give you. Apparently someone sold your father's goods." Mother Laurentia handed me a ten-guilder note. Dully I looked at the words *Dai Nippon Tekoku Seihu*, The Government of Imperial Japan, *Sepoeloeh Roepiah*, Ten Guilders. Only much later did it register that Father must have spent his last money on extra food and sold his Swiss watch. The ten guilders were probably the proceeds of his clothing and bedding.

"Would you like me to stay with you for a while?"

"No, thank you, I'll go and tell Antoinette and Alette. They'll be in the kitchen."

Mother Laurentia left, and I walked down the hill. Alette was stirring rice in a drum with a long stick. When she saw my face, she knew why I had come. "You have bad news about Father, haven't you?" and I said, "Yes."

Antoinette, flapping a fire nearby, said the same thing I had said to Mother Laurentia. "I guess it is our turn."

I can't recall that we showed emotion. We must have been too numb to even feel emotion. The tears and grief for the loss of our beloved father came after the war, when each of us dealt with it in her own private way.

It helped then to learn that Father had died peacefully in his sleep, confident to the end that peace was near, that the Allies would come, that he would be reunited with the three of us and with Mother. When a fellow-internee visited him in a Muntok camp hospital a few days before his death, and suggested that perhaps Father should write or dictate a letter, just in case, Father said there was no reason to already make such preparations. "Your father was one of the most equanimous men in the camp," this man reported. "Thanks to his deep faith and enormous optimism, he did not suffer as much as many others."

🙙 🙙 🙙

I continued to walk zombie-like through the camp, until I finally had to go into the camp hospital with pernicious jaundice caused by the malaria attacks.

One day, quite suddenly, khaki-colored Japanese Army blankets arrived for the sick. Since the little hospital lay at the lowest point of the rubber plantation, it was never touched by the sun and was always dank and musty. We greatly appreciated the blankets, but what did they mean? Could this be a sign that the war was over at last?

On August 24, 1945, it happened. All of us who could walk were summoned to the hill near the guardhouse. I heard in the hospital that Seki, the Japanese camp commander, stood on a table and announced in Malay, "*Perang habis*," the war is over. He did not say who had won, nor that the armistice had been signed nine days before.

"And there we stood," remembers Käty Tekelenburg who was then in her teens. "We felt like a balloon that had been pricked with a needle. You know . . . poof! That was it. I had imagined that we'd explode into an expression of joy. But it didn't happen. It was very curious."

Oh, there *were* expressions of joy. The Dutch sang "The Wilhelmus," and the British and Australians sang "God Save the King." A Dutch woman pulled out a Dutch flag and hung it from her barrack roof. Women pulled out tiny hoards of food and cooked delectable, filling meals for themselves and friends. And more food came in. All those staples that were supposed to have been in short supply outside the camp now arrived in unbelievable quantities: sugar, butter, rice, meat, *kacang hijau*, bananas, even pineapples and papayas and quinine and other medicines, inflatable rings for bedridden patients, bedpans. For many months during the worst dysentery crises, the camp hospital had had only one. I can still hear now, after all these years, the anguished call, "Sister, sister, bedpan!"

Everything we had asked for in three years we now received in three days.

Our men arrived, but many husbands and fathers were missing. Spouses who were reunited looked at each other and didn't know whether to laugh or cry. How dreadful both looked. Children, dressed in the last remaining or quickly made finery or in borrowed clothes, shied away when they saw the bearded scarecrows who were introduced as their fathers. One girl, finding a man sitting at her mother's bedspace and holding her hand, became hysterical. She thought the man was a Japanese soldier and about to harm her mother.

To the camp hospital where I still lay, came a friend of Father's. He brought a Bible Father had somehow obtained and obviously studied. The margins of the pages, mostly in the New Testament, were full of pencil notations in his neat handwriting.

"Sometimes he gave the sermon during Sunday services," said the friend, "and this was always a great comfort to me." With the Bible he also returned the little book of drawings that we had given Father for Christmas, 1942, behind the wire of the houses camp.

Mac, the American journalist, also came to see me in the hospital. And another lifeboat mate came, bearing a Quaker Oats tin filled with boiled liver. "This should be good for that jaundice of yours."

But where were the Allies? No soldiers had stormed the gate yet, as I had pictured our liberation, marching through the camp with flying colors shouting, "Cheer up, girls, your ordeal is over. We've come to take you away!"

Day after day, nothing happened. We were still in the squalid, vermin-infested camp. We still had to cook in sooty drums, although the men now came to help us lift them. Women went right on dying. And we still had to see the Japanese.

At least we didn't have to bow to them anymore and we were spared the daily roll call. And they didn't rush us along with "*Lekas, lekas.*" But from the guardhouse the Japanese flag was still flying. The Japanese had no one to surrender to. British troops assigned to accept the surrender of the 80,000 Japanese troops on Sumatra were still in India. Pending their arrival overseas, the headquarters of the Southeast Asia Command in Colombo, Ceylon sent commando parties of Dutch and British military men to Sumatra to locate the internment and prisoner-of-war camps and to assist with food and medical supplies. Some parties had already been sent by submarine before the Japanese surrender and landed in rubber boats. After the Japanese capitulation, others came by plane and parachuted down. One such team was "Aspect," from the Dutch Special Operations Korps Insulinde. The team consisted of party leader Sargeant-Major C. B. Hakkenberg, *Vaandrig* (Sublieutenant) C. C. Wilhelm, Sargeant J. L. van Hasselt, and the Chinese Ou Chee Suet. They were dropped at Bengkulen on September 5. Not finding camps there, the men radioed Colombo HQ for instructions and were told to "try Lubuklinggau." They drove there in vehicles provided by the Japanese and found our Belalau camp.

The four Dutch paratroopers from "Aspect" were the "Allied troops" we had been waiting for so long. "They were shocked at our accommodations and the way we look," reported Antoinette, "Apparently, other camps are not much better. They have radioed our location to their headquarters, so now the world knows where we are."

A few days later, a few more Allies wandered through the camp. These were Australians, part of a group under British command led by the South African Major G. T. Jacobs and including two men of the Korps Insulinde. The Australians had been searching for weeks for the Australian Army nurses.

The commando teams brought news about the atom bomb. "It killed a hundred thousand people in Hiroshima. All you women may owe your lives to this bomb. A rumor is circulating that the Japanese planned to destroy at least some of the prison camps and their internees before the

Food floats down above the men's camp in Belalau. (Photo courtesy Section Maritime History of the Navy, Department of Defense, The Hague)

surrender. You here were scheduled for annihilation on August 31, Queen Wilhelmina's birthday." I never found out whether this was true. But had the war lasted longer, many more of us internees would have died from illness and starvation.

Food continued to keep coming, and on September 16, the most glorious, most unforgettable food fell from the sky. A huge, light-grey, four-engined plane, called a Liberator, dropped food containers on yellow parachutes over the men's camp. From a cot on which I lay outside the hospital during the day, I watched the plane fly overhead. Not until I saw that huge plane with the red, white, and blue markings of the Dutch Navy instead of the rising sun, did I begin to have a sense that the war was really over.

That afternoon all of us in the women's camp ate slices of buttered bread. It had been baked that morning on the Cocos Islands in the Indian Ocean, where the Liberator had its base—hundreds of kilometers from our camp. According to the plane's log book, the roundtrip flight had taken 10 hours and 55 minutes, and the camp had been difficult to find.

№№   №№   №№

The Australian nurses were the first to leave. The Australian Air Force flew them to Singapore. Here they received medical treatment and were then repatriated to Australia on a hospital ship. The same plane made a second run to Singapore carrying bed-ridden hospital patients.

British non-sick internees, as well as some of the Dutch, were also airlifted to Singapore. Other Dutch, mainly former residents of South Sumatra, were evacuated by train to Palembang and lodged in houses. This group included the Carolus Borromeus Sisters and their family of camp-orphaned children. Fathers came for them from faraway places where they had been prisoners-of-war, or if the fathers had also died, relatives fetched the children. But a year went by before the last child left the nuns.

Thanks to the early evacuation of the Belalau camp—it was empty by the end of October—we were spared the fate of some of the other internment camps in the Dutch East Indies: as they waited month after month in their squalid camps for repatriation, women and children, were murdered by young extremist Indonesian nationalists. Sukarno had proclaimed the independent republic of Indonesia on August 17, 1945.

I left Belalau for Singapore with a transport of ambulatory hospital patients.

It was just getting light when one of the hospital nuns went through the half-empty hospital barrack calling, "The trucks are here. Please get ready." My sisters came to check whether I had everything in my woven-grass bag: eating utensils, mosquito net, and the brand-new Japanese Army blanket.

Also in the bag were camp souvenirs. A scrap of paper said, "Good for one time taking over your wood squad duty." That had been a birthday present from Antoinette. Another scrap read, "Cross your arid desert waste, to the British stronghold. There cement with joy and cheer, links of friend-

179

ship clear and bold." That had been an invitation for the three of us to an "English" party.

With Antoinette and Alette supporting me, I left the camp hospital where I had spent ten weeks, too weak to walk until more food came in. Slowly I shuffled up the muddy path where a partner and I had slithered down with heavy loads of wood, past the barrack where I had slept before going to the hospital, to the guardhouse where I had bowed and said "*Maki wa arimasen,*" there is no wood, to the guard.

Antoinette fussed, "You'd better wear your jacket, it may be chilly when you ride in the truck," and handed me the rice-sack jacket I had made in the first camp. Her eyes took in my thin long legs, my bare feet, and the much-mended camp costume. (My going-away dress and the shoes I had received in the houses camp had been sold.) "Well, you aren't exactly dressed for going away as you had planned, but it doesn't matter, does it?"

Looking back on this long-awaited moment, I realize what an anticlimax our release actually was. That's what I always call it, "release." I never use the word liberation, maybe "liberation in quotes," or our "so-called liberation." There was no glamour or drama attached to the event. It just happened.

Alette cautioned, "Take good care of yourself, and go easy on the sugar." The day before a woman in the camp had died from eating too much sugar.

"Goodbye! See you in Singapore."

I followed a very young, pink-cheeked English soldier who materialized from somewhere. "'Ere you go," he said, and lifted me up onto the truck. "Feathery light you are, dearie." I had already gained a few pounds since the better food came in, but at six feet I still weighed less than 90 pounds.

I rode a train from Lubuklinggau to Lahat, where a plane was waiting at a small airfield. Right under the cockpit were painted in white a pecking swan with spread wings (a squadron designation?) and the letters RAPWI. These stood for Recovery of Allied Prisoners-of-War and Internees.

Then the wheels of the plane thundered over a rough, uneven runway and the wings took us high up, up into the air and away.

At the Singapore airport, fresh-looking, well-coiffed British Red Cross workers in crisp khaki uniforms helped us out of the plane and down the steps. Another young woman in uniform approached with a wheeled cart. She passed around drinks in hygienic-looking paper cups. They were filled with a beige-colored liquid.

"What's this?" I asked, after taking a sip. "It's so sweet."

"It's tea! With sugar and milk."

Apparently, there was sorting to be done. Someone pinned a tag on me, "Johore Hospital," and I was directed toward a bus with other women from my camp so tagged. The vehicle, driven by yet another British girl in uniform, took us to the State of Johore at the southern end of the Malay Peninsula, opposite Singapore. She stopped in front of a modern hospital that the Sultan of Johore had built for his subjects, and that was being used temporarily for care of prisoners-of-war and internees. Lengthy discussions between the bus driver and a white-clad hospital orderly ensued. They consulted the driver's list containing our names. We waited in the bus in resignation. What was another wait after all those years?

The orderly told me to step down. "I'll have to wait here for further instructions for the other patients. Think you can walk to the admission office alone?"

"Oh, yes, I can."

"Go through the door, follow the corridor to the end, turn right. Third door to your left."

I picked up my woven-grass bag and, once I was through the door, held onto the wall and walked to the admission office. Here I found an English nurse with a very big bosom dressed in white. She looked the motherly type, and I hoped she wouldn't treat me as a child, as almost everyone had been doing that day.

"My, what a pretty jacket you're wearing." My heart sank at her cloying tone. Although it had been hot at the airport and hot in the bus, I was still wearing the jacket. It covered my gawky shoulders.

"You'll have to get out of your clothes and give them to me. After you take a shower, I'll give you hospital clothes."

"What will you do with my clothes?"

"We'll boil them. All you internees seem to have lice."

"But you can't boil that jacket. It's made of a rice sack. I sewed it," I almost shrieked.

"Now, don't be upset. You'll get your clothes back . . . if they are salvageable, that is."

I knew I would never see the jacket again. It was the only possession I cared about, and I felt an overwhelming sense of loss. But I mustn't cry, I told myself, I am not a child, I am nearly 25 years old.

I stripped as directed in front of the nurse and felt annoyed that there was no curtain to undress behind. Prewar habits were returning fast.

She handed me a towel and soap and showed me where to take a shower. When I returned, she gave me a hospital sarong and a short gown that smelled of soap and disinfectants, and shoved my clothes into a corner with her shoe. After one last look at the jacket, I followed her to a ward.

My bed had a mattress and a pillow, both with white covers, and a white sheet to sleep under. There was no confining mosquito net, since the windows were screened. The next bed was several feet away.

Through the open window I heard a radio playing unfamiliar Eastern music. Cars drove by. A door slammed. Men and women talked to each other and laughed.

After three-and-a-half years, I was finally out of the camp.

🍃   🍃   🍃

Two weeks later I was discharged and joined my sisters in Singapore's Raffles Hotel. RAPWI had turned this prewar gathering place for the colonial British elite into a reception center for ex-prisoners-of-war and internees. My sisters and I had an enormous room to ourselves, and a maid came in to make the beds.

In the hotel lobby stood a big bowl with tablets of atabrine, a medicine, new (to us) in the treatment of malaria, and free for the taking. In the marble-tiled hallways and up and down the impressive wooden stairs ran gaunt-looking camp children on their bare feet, their just-issued shoes hidden behind a potted palm. Under the gently whirring ceiling fans in the dining room, mothers tried to make their children eat three-course meals with knives and forks and told them not to blow their noses in the napkins.

Relishing the comfort of rattan chairs on the verandah, men and women had their drinks, served again on trays by local waiters, and talked about their spouses.

"My husband was a prisoner-of-war in Burma and worked on that railroad where every sleeper cost the life of a p.o.w. I am expecting him here soon."

"Jim drowned when the Japanese transported p.o.w.'s from here to there on an unmarked ship and Allies bombed the ship."

"My wife and children are still alive on Java, still in their camp."

"I went again to the Red Cross office, but I cannot find out where Joanna is."

At first we couldn't find out where Mother was either. The Allies had divided command over the territories the Japanese were surrendering, and there was as yet not much coordination between the different military groups. Day after day, one of us stood in line with other information seekers at the Red Cross office. Here personnel were compiling lists with names of hundreds of thousands of prisoners-of-war or civilians, already released from or still waiting in camps from Indo-China to Japan.

We passed the days of tormented waiting by acquiring a wardrobe. At a RAPWI clothing center we were issued surplus Australian Army uniforms to wear, everything khaki-colored down to the bras. We hankered for gayer clothes and forayed into the streets, where Indians sold us brightly colored materials and we had dresses made by a Chinese tailor, just as in the olden days. The money for these purchases was handed to us by a Dutch representative of the BPM who had been given instructions by the head office in The Hague "to take care of our people."

Through this paternal figure we finally heard that Mother was alive! She was in an internment camp in Banjermasin, in the south of Borneo, some 2,000 kilometers away.

"But she won't be able to join you yet," he said. "All the internees on Borneo have to stay in their camps until formal repatriation can be arranged."

This gentleman didn't know our mother. Two weeks later, she walked unannounced into our hotel room with a vague tale about an Australian brigadier-general who had helped her to fly to Balik-Papan, and a Dutch bomber pilot who made her sit on the ammunition all the way to Batavia, and yet another pilot who brought her to Singapore. "I think my white hair helped." The last time we saw Mother's hair, it had been brown.

What a joyous and weepy affair this encounter was. We let our emotions go in a way we had not done before—not even when Father and I had met Antoinette and Alette in the jungle of Sumatra, when we were all still traumatized by the shipwreck and the grueling lifeboat voyage.

We talked about Father, whose death Mother had already been told of, and about our respective camps. Mother's had been similar to ours, except it never held more than 120 internees. With so few together, the "camp irritation" tended to be worse than in our larger camp. The women were asked to knit socks for the Japanese, but Mother said she didn't know how to knit. She could not escape, however, mending Japanese officers' uniforms with old Dutch uniform coats.

"But it was easy to make such a coat disappear and use the material for ourselves. I swapped part of a coat for cotton to make a dress, so I didn't have to parade in front of the Japanese in shorts." Mother's camp was also moved several times, and each time conditions became worse.

"Where shall we go now?" asked Mother the next day. "Our home on Tarakan is gone. I think the Allies bombed it when they retook the island, so nothing is to be salvaged there. Without Father holding down a job in the Dutch East Indies, there's nothing to keep us in this part of the world. Anyway, the Dutch are not particularly wanted here at this moment."

Holland didn't seem much of a choice. After five years of German occupation, a huge housing shortage prevailed, and none of our relatives would have room for four guests. Besides, we were not the only members of the family who would be returning from the Dutch East Indies. Two of Mother's brothers and a sister, and Father's two brothers—all with wives and the younger children who had not already been sent to school in Holland—would be repatriating as well.

"What about going to California?" said Mother. She and Father had lived there in the early 1920s. Antoinette and Alette were born there.

We beamed at the suggestion. Antoinette and I were four and five when we left California with our parents and three-week-old Alette for Father's next post on Curaçao in the Caribbean. We had few actual recollections of California, but we had all three leafed through albums of photographs: Helen and Antoinette swimming in an outdoor pool in San Rafael ("You can swim there almost all year," Mother said), holding enormous bunches of grapes, running through sprinklers on what (in the sepia photograph) looked like a lush green lawn, playing on a Santa Monica beach with long strands of seaweed, hiking in the Sierra Nevada. We could well imagine what pleasures California would bring.

California it was.

It took a while to receive U.S. visas for Mother's and my passports,

U.S. passports for American-born Antoinette and Alette, and space on a transatlantic ship. In the meantime, we stayed in a hotel in Richmond-on-the-Thames in England and went to Holland to visit relatives, including Grandmother Colijn.

Grandmother had spent the last three years of the war in Germany, interned with her husband in an Ilmenau hotel, where Grandfather died of a heart attack on September 19, 1944, at the age of 75. Back in The Hague, Grandmother learned that Anton, her eldest of three sons, aged 51, had died in a Japanese internment camp on Sumatra, and Piet, the youngest, 45, was beheaded in Java by the Kenpeitai, the Japanese military police. She had to move into a temporary house, since the red brick mansion on the Stadhouderslaan, a house with so many memories, had been demolished by the Germans to make room for the West wall, a defensive barrier.

We had barely arrived at Grandmother's new residence when Henk was on the phone. He asked me out for dinner. At an elegant restaurant, I received my first marriage proposal. But it had been six years since Henk and I had gone to see the film on the making of the Suez Canal, and I had not heard from him since or thought much about him either. I declined. Grandmother was disappointed, "Such a fine, upright boy."

While waiting for our documents, we began collecting more clothes and things and traveled again with suitcases. At a London station Mother's suitcase must have been too new to resist. Someone took it off the trolley, and with the suitcase went the Bible in which Father had found such solace in the camp.

Gone now were the last mementos of Father's imprisonment. Mother said, "I would have treasured the Bible with his handwriting and the passages that gave him strength, but it would also remind me of him as a prisoner. And I like to think of him free—yodeling on a mountain, skiing down a snowy slope."

❧　❧　❧

In May of 1946, the four of us landed in New York. Friends there helped us to buy a second-hand Dodge, and in it we headed for San Rafael, California, where other friends had invited us to stay with them. Antoinette did most of the driving, having passed an exam for a New York driver's license after failing twice, completely baffled by the lights and the traffic of the big city.

The three of us on a trip to Victoria, British Columbia in 1947

As we left New York on the Pulaski Highway, we turned on the car radio and couldn't believe our ears when we heard a pianist playing Chopin's "Raindrop" Prelude. That was one of the pieces the vocal orchestra had sung during the Christmas concert in 1943. The music seemed a last reminder, a closing off of those terrible years in the internment camp.

For nine days we drove West through towns, past manufacturing plants, along endless fields with wheat and corn, up and down mountains, by enormous lakes. When we were hungry we stopped at roadside cafés, and truck drivers turned around as we trooped in, a white-haired woman with three good-looking daughters in their early twenties, again rosy-cheeked and well-formed. At night we slept in places we had never heard of before: Strasburg, Ohio; Fairbury, Illinois; Lincoln, Nebraska; Wendover, Nevada.

We stayed a month with our friends in San Rafael. They surrounded us with love and treated us to large glasses of orange juice that would have filled half a coconut shell to the brim, slabs of steak as large as the wooden camp sandals called *terompahs*, and other foods in quantities not yet available in war-ravaged England and Holland where we spent the first half-year after our release.

Then the four of us each went separate ways to start a new life in America.

Epilogue

$\mathbb{N}$early 50 years have passed since my mother, sisters, and I made our exhilarating journey by car across the United States. We three girls married, had children and grandchildren, had volunteer or income-earning jobs.

Alette took care of the accounting for a travel agency and later for a medical book publishing company.

Antoinette's activities included thirteen years at what's now called The Lab School of Washington, a school for learning-disabled children. Here she developed and headed the Media Center where children would listen to recorded books, thus exposing them to good children's literature as an incentive to wanting to learn to read. For several years she volunteered for Dr. T. Orin Cornett of Gallaudet College in Washington, learning and applying his system of cued speech for the hearing-impaired. In her spare time she designed and sewed, entirely by hand, dozens of quilted bedspreads and wall-hangings in exuberant colors, which she gives away to family and friends.

After a divorce, I raised a daughter alone. To support us, I translated from Dutch, German, and French for the anatomy department of Stanford University in Palo Alto, California (the subject was prenatal bone growth); tutored high school students in French or German; piloted small groups of teenage American girls through Europe on summer tours I put together; and worked as a staff editor for *Sunset* Magazine.

Our mother, until her death at 95 in 1988, lived close to Alette and me on the San Francisco peninsula. She was a gracious presence in the background who gave advice only if we asked for it and made discreet telephone calls to us about birthdays we should remember. ("I just wrote a note to Aunt Connie, it's already her seventieth birthday.")

When the four of us made that epic journey to California in 1946, we agreed to let bygones be bygones and put the camps behind us. Indeed, we rarely talked about the wartime experiences to each other or to our friends. But then one day in 1980, Antoinette was rummaging in the attic of her Washington home and came upon the 68-page booklet she had put together after the war for her vocal orchestra scores. She hadn't looked at it for years, opened it, and saw to her dismay that the minutely penciled notes had begun to fade. Then and there, she decided to donate the music to a museum or library, so that it could be properly treated and preserved for future generations.

Letting the manuscripts out of her house touched off a string of totally unforeseen events.

The booklet with music found a new home in Stanford University in Palo Alto, California, where it now rests in a custom-made, airtight buckram box in the Department of Special Collections and University Archives in the Green Library. The call number is M147. (Other complete sets of the vocal orchestra music are in the Imperial War Museum in London and the Australian War Memorial in Canberra.)

Stanford was Antoinette's choice because she studied there a year as part of a projected medical career. She also sang in the Memorial Church Choir. "My happiest memory of Stanford."

When the archivist of the university's Archive of Recorded Sound saw the newly acquired music manuscripts, she "ooh-ed" and "aah-ed" and said, "If only a choir could sing some of the pieces so the Archive would have a recording."

The 50-odd singers of the Peninsula Women's Chorus of Palo Alto, California, directed by Patricia Hennings, began rehearsing the vocal orchestra music.

Some found it easy to sing. Others didn't.

"It's difficult to sustain the same syllable. I get tired. I feel my whole body is working at this, trying to put something across along with the singing."

"Without words to tie to the notes . . . especially in the first alto part with often repeated note accompaniment to the melody, it is hard to keep track of where you are in relation to everyone else."

"It's tricky music. Grieg's 'Morning' is no joke. I can't imagine how the women in the camp did it. They weren't even a collection of trained voices, as we are."

"Singing this music is a heavy trip. I get caught up in the emotions about what that camp was like, can't sing without a lump in my throat."

A chorus member who is Australian by birth wrote me, "My father was a member of the ZP Special Force, an Australian secret service group. He was killed in the Dutch East Indies when I was only 15 months old, so I have no memories of him. As a child I used to wonder whether I really ever had a father. This music gives him a reality and a feeling of continuity that I don't think I can explain. I feel that I am singing as a tribute to my father, to my uncle Ken, and three other uncles who fought for Australia."

The 1982 concert, "Music in a Prison Camp—introduced by survivor Helen Colijn," in Annenberg Auditorium at Stanford, was an overwhelming success. "The whole world should hear this," a deeply touched concert-goer said afterward. Her remark planted the seed for a TV documentary.

The hour-long *Song of Survival* film took three-and-a-half years to make, from the conception to the first screening, as long a time as we spent in the camp. Producers were Stephen Longstreth, David Espar, and Robert Moore of Veriations films in Palo Alto, with an assist from me. Financial support came from the National Endowment of the Humanities in Washington, the Netherlands Broadcasting Corporation in Hilversum, private American groups and individuals, including Antoinette and quilting friends who meet every Wednesday. They made a handsome quilted bedspread and raffled it off, "to help make a movie," as posters in a shopping mall announced.

We shot the documentary in The Netherlands where we organized a reunion of eighty of the "camp children," in Indonesia, where we visited the last camp site in Belalau, and in Menlo Park, California. In 1983, nine of the surviving original vocal orchestra singers flew in from The Netherlands, Great Britain, Australia, Indonesia, and across the United States to attend what was now called a *Song of Survival* concert presented by the Peninsula Women's Chorus. Several of the guests had not seen each other since release from the Belalau camp in 1945.

There they were sitting, the nine guests, in a front pew of St. Bede's church in Menlo Park to hear the music they sang so long ago, under such dire circumstances. They wore rose corsages. They wore dresses and shoes. Their gray heads were beautifully coiffed. Although I had sent them all tapes of the previous year's concert, this was the first time they had heard their music live.

Norah Chambers was tapping a fist in her hand, keeping time with the music and shaking her head, as if to say, "No, that isn't the way I did it at all." At times, her face crumpled and tears came to her eyes. Later she told me she was seeing her battered singers in the camp, about half of whom died before release.

Antoinette looked drawn, too. The music must be evoking sad memories, I thought, as I watched her. I was sitting in the pew with the camp singers. Next to me, Sister Catharinia was beaming. She loved the music for what it was, and was not thinking of the camp at all, she told me.

At the end of the program the chorus sang The Captives' Hymn. At the first words we ten from the camp stood. Hesitantly, not knowing what was expected, others in the church rose. By the end of the first verse the entire audience was standing. Chorus members had tears in their eyes. Patricia Hennings, with her back to the audience, wondered just what was going on.

The documentary premiered in The Netherlands in 1985, in the United States in 1986 and has since been shown again or anew in other countries as well. It is available for home video in the United States, and in Japan with Japanese subtitles. Distribution in Japan by Tokyovision is for educational and library use. Atsushi Takahashi of Tokyovision wrote me that he was a boy during the war in the industrial city of Nagoya. Nagoya was bombed and many of its citizens died. He witnessed the horror of war, watching many dogfights, Kamikaze suicide attacks, and houses burning to

In the 1980s internees Betty Jeffrey of Australia (left) and Sigrid Stronk of The Netherlands recalled the camp. "Conditions in the camp were terrible," noted Betty, "terrible all the time, but you did make the best of it." Sigrid felt "We were privileged to have children. To have something to really live for." (Photo of Betty Jeffrey by Doug Mecham)

ashes. He came to believe that war is not a solution to resolving conflict and decided to do his best to work for peace in our world.

The next phase in the ever expanding project was the publication of sheet music for several of the vocal orchestra pieces by Universal Songs in The Netherlands. In 1995 the Dutch Vrouwenkoor Malle Babbe (Women's Choir of Haarlem) directed by Leny van Schaik released the CD Song of Survival. The music and the story of the women captured the imagination of Australian film director Bruce Beresford, who directed the film *Paradise Road* starring Glenn Close. The Malle Babbe choir sings the Song of Survival music on the soundtrack of the film, which is being distributed by Sony Classical on CD and cassette. In the planning stages are a *Song of Survival* play, a drama with choral music, written by Ray and Eleanor Harder of Los Angeles for use in schools and churches.

Now that the vocal orchestra music and the story behind it are traveling over the world via air waves and satellites, on videotapes and CDs, in printed articles and books, survivors, including those who chose to bury all

191

Norah Chambers (British) speaking of the vocal orchestra concerts: "In spite of all the smells and muck and goodness knows what, we literally forgot where we were."

memories, are asked probing questions. Answers are as varied as are the women and the children old enough at the time to remember the camp.

Take the question, "How do you feel about the Japanese?" In 50 years, most survivors have mellowed. Only a few are still torn up by hatred, turn off the television set if Japanese persons come on the screen, and refuse to buy Japanese products. Others have traveled to Japan and enjoyed it, have befriended Japanese persons or persons of Japanese descent, and welcomed them into their families.

My own healing process began with a trip to San Francisco to interview a Japanese official for a *Sunset* story on travel in Japan that I was working on. I dreaded the rendezvous: the first Japanese I had met since the war. To my relief, I found shaking hands with him no different from shaking hands with an American or Dutchman. It helped, perhaps, that he was as tall as I, and he spoke English with barely an accent. In no way did he resemble one of the small guards in the camp barking orders in an unintelligible tongue. He was so young, obviously born after the war, so I could hardly hold him responsible for the behavior of an older generation.

Then I saw a program on television about an elderly Japanese man who wore a floppy grey hat and liked to look at brush paintings. The

Sister Catharinia (Dutch) speaking of the vocal orchestra concerts: "It was something that lived between us, and it made us more near together, that was the wonder of the music."

announcer introduced him as Hirohito, the emperor of Japan. You are looking at the man you bowed to for three years in the camp, I thought. I had never seen his picture. This meeting with the emperor in my own living room seemed totally incongruous. Here he was, just a little old man. Alone in my living room, I laughed out loud.

Around that time, in the early 1980s, I met more Japanese people. In a local bookstore, a Japanese gentleman, I believe associated with Stanford University, was browsing near me when I took a copy of *The Chrysanthemum and the Sword* from the shelf. I thought reading up on Ruth Benedict's perceptive book on patterns of Japanese culture might help blow away anti-Japanese feelings. With courtesy, the browser then said, "If you are interested in Japan, perhaps you will like reading *The Harp of Burma*." He wrote down the name of the author, Michio Takayama, and as a curiosity for me, the title in Japanese characters. I later bought a copy and after reading the first paragraph about the Japanese soldiers coming back form overseas—looking thin, weak, exhausted—I became enthralled:

> Among the returning soldiers there was one company of cheerful men. They were always singing, even difficult pieces in several parts, and they sang very well. When they disembarked at Yokosuka, the people who came to greet them were astonished. Everyone asked if they had received extra rations, since they seemed so happy. These men had no extra rations, but had practiced choral singing throughout the Burma campaign. Their captain, a young musician fresh from music school, had enthusiastically taught his soldiers how to sing. It was singing that had kept up their morale through boredom or hardship, and that bound them together in friendship and discipline during the long war years.

Here I was reading a story about the Japanese being uplifted by music, just as we were in the camp, led by a captain who, like Margaret Dryburgh, must have said something like, "Sing, Thou will be happier," and, like Norah Chambers, taught his group to sing, probably "teaching the notes first, and them starting to 'put in color, light, and shade, slow or fast, that sort of thing.'"

Shortly thereafter, still in connection with the *Sunset* story, I met Tomoko Nakamura, then working in San Francisco on the staff of the North American Japanese newspaper *Hokubai Mainichi*. She had also read *The Harp of Burma*, required reading in her Tokyo high school. I told her about the vocal orchestra, and we talked about music and the war—as friends. The year after we met, she sent me a card. It showed sheer curtains blown by wind through an open window. Tomoko wrote on the card, "For your memories," and signed it with her name and date, August 15th, the date the war between the U.S. and Japan ended. Enclosed with the card from Japan, where she had returned, was a tiny origami bird she had folded. For several years after that, I received a card from Japan in August, always with one or more of those tiny origami birds.

With regard to feelings about the Japanese, Mother tells in the *Song of Survival* film that the last thing my father said to her on Tarakan, before the Japanese took him away as a hostage, was, "'Whatever happens to you, don't feel bitter about it, because bitterness will destroy you' . . . and I didn't. That was his last gift to me."

Not to feel bitter, to forgive is a difficult task.

Survivors of the South Sumatra camp find the task is made easier by the knowledge that out of our ugly place came beautiful music that now brings joy and solace to other singers and listeners around the world.

Margaret Dryburgh at her graduation in 1911. (Photo courtesy United Reformed Church, London)

Profile of
Margaret Dryburgh

In the camp we saw the vocal orchestra music as just another way of making something out of nothing, of making do with what we had, not as the amazing feat that people saw it for in later years, nor as material that would become the subject of articles and books. Had we ever given such a possibility a thought, we might have asked Miss Dryburgh what musical training she had, where she had heard all that music she remembered, how she remembered it.

Those are the kinds of questions people ask now, and we survivors also ask them as we look back in wonder. Now we, too, find Margaret Dryburgh's talent amazing. Here she was, already imprisoned a year and a half, and *from memory* she wrote down piano and orchestral scores she hadn't heard for who knows how long. Then she and Norah Chambers condensed the scores and rearranged them for voices without losing the harmonic and linear aspects of the original instrumental parts, all without a music book or a musical instrument as a guide.

In the 1980s, I set out to find answers to the questions not asked in the camp. I wrote letters to friends and former students of Miss Dryburgh's in

197

England and Singapore, but didn't find out as much about her musical background as I had hoped. However, my contacts did provide other information.

Born in 1890 in Sunderland in northern England, the child of a Presbyterian minister, little Margaret played the piano at home, as did her mother and two sisters, who called Margaret Daisy.

In 1911, she graduated with a B.A. from Newcastle College, then a division of Durham University, having studied education and music.

Her first teaching post was at Ryhope Grammar Girls' School, where she led the school choir. About this period, one of her students wrote to me in 1983:

> Miss Dryburgh was gentle and kind. She must have been 21 or 22. To me she was 'grown-up' and as a teacher someone in a special category. Only now I realize how modest and unassuming she was. She taught Latin and History—to be frank, not very well . . . instead she often gave us 'pious talk,' —pi-jaw to the less devout. I cannot remember whom she talked of, but I do remember tears in the eyes—hers or mine or both because she was so earnest. Also, I still have the autograph album which was the fashion while I was at school. The staff, each one, duly wrote a signature in my album. Miss Dryburgh, to my amazement and delight, painted a lovely water color—a moonlit scene in sepia. I have never been able to decide what led her to expend so much time on a silly schoolgirl. Perhaps it was her nature that when she gave, she gave her whole self.

A few months after I received this letter, I called on this former student in a retirement home amid the moors of Cumbria. On her bedside table lay the autograph book and a razor blade and a ruler. She invited me to remove Margaret Dryburgh's moonlit scene and take it home with me to California, where it now hangs framed on a wall.

The small water color is signed, "With best wishes, M. Dryburgh, March 1914." It shows the kind of lateen-rigged dhows one sees in the Orient. Was Margaret Dryburgh already longing to leave for China to begin her planned missionary work? She had to wait for this until the end of World War I.

From 1919 to 1925, she worked for the English Presbyterian mission in Swatow, South China. Already the able organizer we came to know in the camp, she supervised the schools attached to churches in villages and towns throughout the Swatow district. A woman who attended the Sok Tek school (the words mean Pertaining to Moral Excellence) wrote recently, "All of the schoolmates admired this teacher. She was very bright and quick. Transferring a music diagram to romanization (do re mi fa sol), she just spent a few seconds to finish the work."

When the mission churches in South China suffered persecution because of their association with capitalist countries, the EPM staff had to leave. Margaret Dryburgh went to Singapore to work among the Teochow Chinese, whose language she spoke fluently. They called her Beautiful Pearl—the name Margaret means Pearl.

In Singapore she is still remembered as an organist in the Presbyterian church on Orchard Road (she played to earn money for printing Sunday School and Bible studies at her Chinese church) and as the first principal of the Kuo Chuan Girls' School. This school exists now as the Kuo Chuan Presbyterian Secondary School on Bishan Street.

A Chinese woman who was a teacher at the old school reported, "Miss Dryburgh could be quick-tempered, but her anger was usually short-lived, and she never failed to apologize." A student wrote, "She was an absolutely outstanding character, great and grand, a dynamic human force."

This former Sok Tek student also sent me a tribute she found in *Working His Purpose Out—History of the English Presbyterian Mission (1847-1947)*, published by the Presbyterian Church of England Publishing Office in London (year unknown). The book includes Miss Dryburgh's years in Singapore, then part of Malaya. "M. Dryburgh gave of her abilities without stint to the Chinese Church, training teachers and Bible women, visiting and up-building. Perhaps her greatest gift to the church in Malaya came from what was a central force in her own life, a love of music. Music to her was both an inspiration and a way of expressing the joy and glory of the Christian faith, and this she passed on to choirs and schools and congregations so that those who have known the church in Malaya speak of it as a 'singing church.'"

Where did Margaret Dryburgh first hear complex orchestral works used for the vocal orchestra like, for instance, the Largo from the *New World* symphony? We can only guess. Maybe a local or guest orchestra gave a concert in Singapore and Miss Dryburgh attended. Or she might have been given a gramophone record and then played it on a Victrola in the mission house. She probably played the piano pieces herself, or had them played to her over and over again by her piano students. "Jesu, Joy" and Handel's Pastorale must have been favorite pieces on the organ of the Orchard Road church. And she might have played piano arrangements of orchestral classics.

And how did she manage, after "probing" her memory, to recall with hardly any errors all those scores from classical masters?

Did Margaret Dryburgh have a photographic memory to help her remember the musical scores? She may well have had such a memory, as, at age seven, she received a first prize at the Synod Scripture Examination at the Presbyterian Church at Swalwell, where her father was then a minister. A photographic memory would have helped her memorize the texts, and later musical scores. But when I discussed this with Norah Chambers shortly before her death in 1989, Norah dismissed the idea, "Margaret carried the sounds of the music in her head, not a picture of the printed scores."

As for the melody of "The Captives' Hymn," some time ago K. Marie Stolba, Professor of Music, Emerita, at Indiana University-Purdue University, looked at the lines phrase by phrase. She thinks that the arrangement is composed of fragments of hymn melodies Miss Dryburgh knew and loved. (The hymn's words are on page 105.) The hymn is now sung at the end of vocal orchestra concerts. Sometimes it is sung by a mixed choir in Margaret Dryburgh's SATB arrangement. Sometimes a church congregation or concert audience is invited to sing along with a choir.

One wishes that Miss Dryburgh could have known how many people, long after the camp, would be touched by her hymn. And one wishes she could have heard the beautiful vocal orchestra music from the outside. As she sang in the vocal orchestra she could only hear the music from within. But with her wonderful musical talent, she doubtless correctly imagined the music as it would sound to a listener in the audience.

More Information

Instead of weaving more informative details into the text or adding footnotes or endnotes, I have included this supplementary material. Subjects appear in the order in which they are first mentioned in the text.

Chapter One

The Netherlands East Indies may be more familiar as the Dutch East Indies. At the time of my story, the Indies were still a colony of the Kingdom of The Netherlands, a tiny country that fits 13 times into the state of California. The Indies on the other hand, consisting of some 13,000 islands and seas in between, covered 5 million square kilometers. If you were to place the archipelago on the USA, it would reach from California to Bermuda.

The islands became a Dutch colony in the beginning of the nineteenth century. But for two centuries before that they were already sites for Dutch trading posts where the early Dutch merchants bought spices. Mace, cloves, and pepper enriched the merchants and the Dutch government that had the trading monopoly. Later the Dutch gathered wealth with coffee, tea and rubber, and later yet with oil.

In 1948 the Netherlands East Indies became the independent republic of Indonesia.

The four largest islands of Indonesia are, in alphabetical order: Java, Kalimanten (formerly called Borneo), Sulawesi (formerly Celebes), and Sumatra where most of the action of *Song of Survival* takes place.

Sumatra is 1750 kilometers long and up to 400 kilometers wide. About one third consists of swampy area lying along most of the east coast. An unbroken mountain range, the Bukit Barisan mentioned in chapter five, and steamy jungles stretch along the length of the west coast.

The governor-general was the highest government authority when the Indies were still part of the Kingdom of The Netherlands. He represented the monarch in The Netherlands. At the outbreak of the war with Japan in 1941 the monarch was Queen Wilhelmina in exile in London because Nazi Germany had occupied The Netherlands the year before. The governor-general, or G.G., was Jhr. Mr. A. W. J. Tjarda van Starkenborgh Stachouwer. *Jhr.* stands for *Jonkheer*, a title of nobility, and *Mr.* indicates a Dutch law degree.

Malay was the common language between the many diverse peoples of the islands, all peoples speaking languages of their own. Malay also often was the language of communication between the local population and the Dutch settlers.

When the colony became an independent republic, Malay became the official language of the republic and is now called Indonesian.

Current spelling of Indonesian differs from the spelling of Malay in colonial times. For example, the "oe" has been replaced by "u," the "tj" by a "c." Except for the name of the ship that sank, *Poelau Bras*, I have spelled all Malay words we used with the Indonesian spelling of today. That's how you'll find those words now spelled in dictionaries. The one I used was *An Indonesian-English dictionary* by Echols and Shadily, third edition, published by Cornell University Press, 1989.

Place names in this book appear as you will find them spelled on current maps.

Alette's high school was a *lyceum*, one of several types of high schools then in use in The Netherlands and in the Dutch East Indies. Each type of school offered a curriculum leading to different career objectives. A twelve-year old leaving a six-year grade school and earmarked to be a lawyer or a physician requiring a university degree would go to a different high school than a girl or boy aspiring to be a skilled mechanic requiring a trade school diploma. Since the war, the Dutch school system has undergone radical changes. A school by the name of lyceum no longer exists, but the variety in types of high school still does.

CHAPTER TWO

The *Poelau Bras*, with her captain P. G. Crietée on board, sank at 10° south latitude/105° east longitude. A Dutch book, *Nederlandse Zeeman's Graven* (Dutch Seaman's Graves), compiled in Nijmegen in 1987 by Ed Melis and Wil van Hamel for the Foundation Commemorative Junyo Maru— Sumatra, lists some 40 Dutch naval and merchant vessels sunk by Japanese torpedoes or bombs, with a loss of nearly 3,000 lives, during the three months the Japanese fought for and conquered the Netherlands East Indies.

CHAPTER THREE

Red talks about "the whites." This word is now frowned upon, but I have retained it in speech of the time. Because that's the way we talked about ourselves, and the word whites is not an ugly word. But I have avoided the word "natives" we used when talking about the local population. That word now is offensive to the population groups concerned. For the same reason I have cleaned up my own or other people's speech when calling the Japanese Japs or other unflattering nicknames. The war with Japan has now been over for 50 years, and hauling out ephithets uttered in anger, grief, or frustration in the past contributes nothing towards building a lasting peace. So in this book the Japanese are called Japanese except for a few instances of dialogue where the use of Japanese would not convey the attitudes of the war period.

My *gymnasium*, like Alette's *lyceum*, opened the way to university studies, but had a six-year curriculum whereas the lyceum had a five-year one. So far, the gymnasium has survived the Dutch changes in education.

CHAPTER FIVE

The speed with which people were interned in other places in the Dutch East Indies varied. On Java, for example, "internment took place step-by-step and was not completed till the middle of 1943. This was partly due to the large number of allied civilians, partly to the personal opinion of the Japanese military commander, who considered undue haste unnecessary and inhumane. He needed, moreover, many of these allied civilians for the restoration of economic life on the island." From the standard Dutch work entitled *Japanse Burgerkampen* (Japananese Camps for Civilians) by Dr. Dora van Velden, published in 1973. She was herself interned in the notorious Tjideng camp in Batavia with 10,000 women and children.

Back in Holland, Dora van Velden planned to write a doctoral thesis about her camp, but ended up compiling a book about all the women's camps, and all the men's camps, and in a few cases joint camps in the Dutch East Indies, but also about all the civilian camps in Japan, Korea, Manchuria, China, Indo-China, Thailand, Hong Kong, Burma, Singapore, Australian New Guinea and on some Pacific Islands as well. An English summary will be helpful to those who don't read Dutch but does not convey the high quality of the book nor the wise and compassionate insights of the author.

CHAPTER SIX

After the war, ***our system of kongsis*** of varying size who cooked for themselves drew the following comment from British Captain Jennings, husband of Margery Jennings in our camp.

"Our women suffered untold hardships bravely and with amazing fortitude, but I gather there was complete lack of internal discipline as compared with a military camp. Ten women would 'dine' in a little group here, and six women there. If the ten got any extras, they did not share them with the six. Each gang had its own little fire. There was no communal feeding as with us."

Captain Jennings spent several years in a Japanese camp for prisoners-of-war. The quote is part of a collection of correspondence and other documents from the Archives of the United Reformed Church in London and transferred to the Archives of the Library of the School of African and Oriental Studies of the University of London.

A third often advanced ***reason for our internment*** was one we only heard about after the war: internment of all the Dutch—100,000 or so—and nationals from other Allied countries in the Dutch East Indies was a reprisal for the internment of 110,000 people of Japanese ancestry in the Western states of the U.S.

Historians, however, point out that President Roosevelt signed Executive Order 9066 on February 19, 1942. This order gave the War Department authority to define military areas in the western states and to exclude from them anyone who might threaten the war effort, and led to the internment of Japanese-Americans. By February 19, 1942, the Japanese had already started interning Dutch nationals in the Dutch East Indies (on Tarakan, for example), going full-speed ahead after the Dutch colony capitulated to Japan on March 9, 1942.

Creating a semblance of a previous life no doubt helped us women to endure and gave us an advantage over interned men—the civil servants, teachers, planters, businessmen cooped up for two to three years in camps like ours.

Dora van Velden observes in her book that cooking, washing, cleaning, and taking care of children were normal activities for most of the women, even if they had had servants before the camp. They didn't think it beneath their dignity to do these things, as a large number of men did. Typically, only once in a while, with much aversion would a male prisoner rinse a pair of shorts under a tap or in a river. Women had the tendency to make their camp homes as cozy as possible. Men often didn't. The author further mentions how women had a better chance at survival because they were more flexible. The women didn't mind as much having to adjust to the presence and will of others. In their homes this had been expected of them as natural. The men had a tendency to neglect routine jobs or do nothing at all. They didn't seem to care, for instance, how they looked or what language they used.

Malay also was the common language in the camp between "the English" who didn't speak Dutch (most of them) and the Dutch who didn't speak English (several of them). Both groups knew at least some Malay from talking with their servants. Some Malay words became part of everyone's camp vocabulary and part of this book.

balai	couch
balai-balai	plural, in camp used for sleeping platform
djemur	dry in the sun
gaplék	dried cassava, tapioca

gedék	plaited bamboo
gula jawa	Javanese sugar (from *arén* or sugar palm)
jemur	dry in the sun
kabar angin	"wind news" (communication between locals)
kangkung	kind of spinach
kacang hijau	small, green (*hijau*) pea
Kenpetai	Japanese military police
kongsi	commercial assocation, partnership, used in camp for (cooking) group
lekas	quick(ly)
pendopo	or *pendapa*, used in camp for small open pavilion (hut) in compound
pici	rimless cap, usually of black velvet, worn by Muslims
sambal	chili pepper paste
tempat	place, used in camp for bed space, "home"
terompah	wooden sandal with strap over toes
ubi kaju	cassava

The Japanese words that became part of camp jargon were few:

arigato	thank you
Hei-ho	soldier of local militia in Japanese service
Nippon	Japan
samurai	class of military men dating back to feudal times
tenko	counting

CHAPTER SEVEN

Theo Rottier, one of the children who saw the **man being tortured** told me a few years ago, "This thing has been haunting me for years. Whenever I saw someone on TV being hit I switched the channel or closed my eyes. It made me sick. In 1973, I deliberately went back to the houses camp, stood on the very spot where this man died, and took a photograph hoping to lay to rest the traumatic experience of seeing the man slowly die."

The **removal of young boys**, sometimes as young as ten, was the rule in all women's camps in the Dutch East Indies. Many boys were still children, as the mothers claimed. One of them went off to the men's camp with a teddy bear in his backpack, and when he found other young boys there, they asked each other, "Have you cried yet?" This is an anecdote in Henk Leffelaar's book, *Through a Harsh Dawn—A Boy Grows up in a Japanese Prison Camp.* He was sent from a women's camp on North Sumatra to a men's camp where he didn't find his father, who was a prisoner-of-war in Burma, and was assigned a "camp uncle."

The mothers' concerns about young boys in a men's camp were valid. Dora van Velden writes that "in all men's camps one thought it was better to lodge the boys in separate barracks because of the bad influence which might exude from the men."

CHAPTER EIGHT

Cessation of menstruation, we learned years later, is extremely common and is frequently related to emotional trauma such as divorce, unemployment or other stressful situations. Menstruation usually returns in a few months without treament. In our case we had to wait three years for the return of a normal monthly cycle. We felt its absence was one of the best things that happened to us in the camp.

CHAPTER TEN

The hand-written original of **Margaret Dryburgh's introduction to the first vocal orchestra concert** is in the Department of Special Collections and University Archives, Stanford University Libraries in Stanford, California.

Norah Chambers told her singers to sing the final chords of the Largo with a sound of triumph, "you are singing for victory."

A Dutch woman told me recently that her mother had *a book of popular piano pieces* in the camp. In it were Schumann's "Dreaming" and Brahms "Waltz No. 15," both sung by the vocal orchestra. It could be, then, that Margaret Dryburgh consulted this book before or while writing down the pertinent vocal orchestra scores. But the woman doesn't recall Margaret borrowing the book, nor does anyone in her barrack recall ever seeing Margaret with a piano book in hand to refresh her astonishing memory.

CHAPTER ELEVEN

The 37% *death rate* figure is taken from Dora van Velden's book on Japanese camps for civilians. She writes in a foreword to the Dutch edition of *Song of Survival* that in no other camps in the Netherlands East Indies did the death rate come even close to this figure, except for a small men's camp in Menado where almost half of the internees died.

Were these *moves from camp to camp* planned by someone in Tokyo to crush our morale? Each move was a setback for us, and in each we had to leave behind precious belongings, including in this particular instance the *ubi kaju*'s we had planted in the compound with so much sweat and muscle aches. The sweet potatoes were not yet ready to be harvested.

And the new surroundings were always worse than the ones we left behind. Often kongsis, which supported each other even if they couldn't cook together anymore, had to be broken up owing to space demands. With every move, a carefully nurtured sense of camp security was destroyed: a new "home" had to be built, new personal spaces established by means of a partitioning cloth or a picture of a family member, and new people had to be adjusted to.

All the women's camps on Sumatra, Java, Borneo, and Celebes—some twenty at the end of the war with roughly sixty thousand women and children—report the same conditions. It seemed as if it would have been relatively easy for the Japanese to make those wretched transports a bit less wretched, to alleviate the crowded housing conditions by building additional huts, and to provide medicines and more food. The Japanese arguments at the time were that better means of transport were not available, nor were medicines and adequate supplies of food.

CHAPTER TWELVE

How Father would have liked to climb Mont Blanc with us. He loved the mountains. Whenever he was to be transferred by Shell, he would look at a map and say, "That's good, we can go climbing in . . . (Venezuela, Rumania), and when he was to be transferred to New Guinea he was elated because he would be near mountains that had never been climbed at all.

In 1936 Father and two other Dutchmen made a *first ascent of the Ngga Pulu*, a fifteen-thousand-foot glacier-covered mountain in the

Carstenz Mountains. Where previous expeditions had failed because their assault parties had been too cumbersome (a hundred or more porters and military escorts) and lasted too long (six to nine months) and didn't have alpine equipment, Father and his two climbing partners made a two-month trip with eleven Dayak porters from Borneo and ice axes and crampons. Father wrote a book about the expedition, *Naar de eeuwige sneeuw van tropisch Nederland* (To the Eternal Snow of the Tropical Netherlands), reissued after the war with the title, To the Eternal Snow of New Guinea.

CHAPTER THIRTEEN

The title page of **Sumatran Diary** states "compiled from notes kept by Margaret Dryburgh, B.A., a Presbyterian Missionary of Singapore. While escaping, with three colleagues, she was interned in Sumatra from 1942-1945." No publisher, date or place of issuance are mentioned.

EPILOGUE

The two books cited, Ruth Benedict's *The Chrysanthemum and the Sword*, on Japanese culture patterns, first issued in 1946, and Michio Takeyama's fictional *Harp of Burma*, first issued in 1966, were still in print at the time this book went to press.

For a reader interested in other books about the camps I was in, there is Betty Jeffrey's diary *White Coolies*, first issued in Australia in 1954, reissued since then in close to forty different editions, and Lavinia Warner's and John Sandiland's *Women Beyond the Wire*, a third-person account based on extensive interviews with primarily British internees, issued in London in 1982.

ADDRESSES FOR OTHER SONG OF SURVIVAL RESOURCES

Song of Survival 58-minute documentary
>Janson Associates
>88 Semmens Road
>Harrington Park, NJ 07640
>Phone: 1-800-952-6766 Fax: 1-201-784-3993

Published Song of Survival scores
>BMG Music Publishing
>1 Music Circle N., Suite 380
>Nashville, TN 37203
>Phone: 1-615-780-5420 Fax: 1-615-780-5430

Vol. 1: The Captives' Hymn for women's voices; Largo from Dvořák's From the New World; Jesu, Joy of Man's Desiring
Vol. 2: Christmas Medley (including *Messiah* pastorale)
Vol. 3: Chopin prelude no. 20, "Funeral March"; Beethoven minuet Bolero; Londonderry Air
Vol. 4: To a Wild Rose; Auld Lang Syne; Country Gardens; Faery Song
Vol. 5: Third movement Mozart sonata KV 545; Andante cantabile, Tchaikovsky string quartet
Vol. 6: "Morning," Grieg Peer Gynt suite; Chopin prelude no. 15, "Raindrop"

On a separate sheet, The Captives' Hymn SATB

Unpublished Song of Survival scores
>Universal Songs B.V.
>P.O. Box 2305
>1200 CH Hilversum, The Netherlands
>Phone: (0) 35-23-16-80 Fax: (0) 35-23-46-48

Song of Survival Recordings
>Available from Sony Classical or contact White Cloud Press

For further information, contact White Cloud Press:
>P.O. Box 3400, Ashland, Oregon 97520
>Phone/fax: 1-800-380-8286

Acknowledgments

This *Song of Survival* book is based on a manuscript I worked on in the 1940s while memories of the shipwreck, the jungle trek, and the ensuing internment were still fresh. When the manuscript was almost finished, I abandoned it in a drawer and did not look at it again until the 1980s. The factual information in that early manuscript then came in handy for a television documentary, for text to go with published music scores, for jackets of recordings, all bearing the *Song of Survival* name, and for my book in Dutch.

Many people and organizations helped to bring about these early incarnations of the *Song of Survival* story. I'd like to thank them here for filling in details, extending financial help, giving editorial advice, and providing photo material, all of which was helpful when I finally sat down to rewrite the old manuscript for the book. The following list also includes names of supporters who have since died.

Nell Abdulkadir (Indonesia); Zus Colijn, Mary Ager, Ronald Bailey, Minco de Bruin, Suzanne Lipsett, Agnes Michaels, Johan van Leer, and K. Marie Stolba (USA); Ai Lan Yeo, Mrs. E. K. Lim, Vivian Statham, Wilma

Young, Betty Jeffrey, Mickey Syers, Flo Trotter, and Cara Kelson (Australia); Ietje Bast, Jacques Dozy, Peggy Feierabend, Sister Catharinia, Kees Hakkenberg, Jan Koot, Dirk Jan Warnaar, Carel Wilhelm, and Nel de Bert (The Netherlands); Mollie Chalmers, Celia Downward, Bill Fletcher, Norah Chambers, Shelagh Lea, and Jessie Hayes (England); Mrs. J. C. Chen and Mrs. Yap (Singapore); Dutch Broadcasting Corporation NOS, which funded part of the documentary; Alette Douglas, Stephen Goodell (USA), who wrote the proposal that led to National Endowment of the Humanities funding of the documentary; Ellen Grooten in The Netherlands who helped locate the "camp children" for the 1984 reunion and some eighty camp children who attended the reunion in The Netherlands and filled out questionnaires; Patricia Hennings (USA) who directed the Peninsula Women's Chorus in the first postwar concert of vocal orchestra music; Ulrich Kappler (Switzerland); and Bram Keizer of Universal Songs in The Netherlands who published several of the vocal orchestra works.

Stephen Longstreth, who with his Veriation Films partners, Robert Moore and David Espar, produced the *Song of Survival* documentary; William Peter Mahrt, E. John Schonleber, Paul van der Veur, Jeanette Zweede, Marlene Mayo, and Hazelle Miloradovitch (USA); Margaret Maltby and Betty Pryce-Jones, nieces of Margaret Dryburgh (England); Jopie de Man, Theo Rottier, Madelyn van Rijckevorsel, Bob Tromp, Shell International, Maritime History of the Navy Section, Department of Defense, National Institute for War Documentation, and Museon (The Netherlands); Antoinette Mayer and her quilting group, and the many other organizations and individuals who donated money towards production of the documentary (USA); Tomoko Nakamura, Atsushi Takahashi, and Kimihiro Yamada, (Japan); Audrey Owen (New Zealand); Käty Resegotti (Switzerland); Leny van Schaik (The Netherlands), who directed the Women's Choir of Haarlem singing for the *Song of Survival* compact disc recording; Stanford University Libraries, Department of Special Collections and University Archives (USA); The United Reformed Church, London (England); War Graves Foundation (The Netherlands and Indonesia); and Irene Levendig (Canada).

I also would like to thank members of choirs in the USA and Australia I heard from who sang the *Song of Survival* music in concerts and thus helped carry the lovely sounds from a dismal prison camp out into the world: Mother McAuley High School Chorus (Chicago); Oral Roberts

University Women's Chorus (Oklahoma); Pembroke Girls Choir (Adelaide, Australia); Peninsula Women's Chorus (California); Portsmouth Women's Chorus (New Hampshire); Santa Fe Women's Choir (New Mexico); Song of Survival Choir (Perth, Australia); Toledo Seaway Chapter of Sweet Adelines (Ohio); West Bend High School Choir (Wisconsin); White Fish Bay High School Choir (Wisconsin); Women of Shadyside Presbyterian Church & Chatham College Choir (Pittsburgh, Pennsylvania); Young Womens Ensemble (Jay, Maine).

I end these acknowledgments with very special thanks to the people who helped put the book together: Colleen Huston who cheerfully re-typed my drafts, mastering all the wonderful intricacies of the computer which to date have eluded me, and also took over some of the research; Sheri Spicklemire who fine-tuned my text; Bill Cheney who designed the cover for the book's Dutch edition and Daniel Cook who modified the design for the English edition; Alice Grulich-Jones who took the author's photo; and Steven Scholl and Janice Lineberger of White Cloud Press. They brought an unbounded enthusiasm to this publication process which made working with them a joy.

Index